55 ways

TO THE WILDERNESS
IN SOUTHCENTRAL ALASKA

55 ways

TO THE WILDERNESS
IN SOUTHCENTRAL ALASKA

By Helen Nienhueser and Nancy Simmerman

Photographs by Nancy Simmerman,
Helen and Gayle Nienhueser and John Ireton

THE MOUNTAINEERS and
MOUNTAINEERING CLUB OF ALASKA

Third edition

THE MOUNTAINEERS. . . . Organized 1906
To explore and study the mountains, forests, and watercourses of the Northwest;
To gather into permanent form the history and traditions of this region;
To preserve by the encouragement of protective legislation or otherwise the
    natural beauty of Northwest America;
To make expeditions into these regions in fulfillment of the above purposes;
To encourage a spirit of good fellowship among all lovers of outdoor life.

MOUNTAINEERING CLUB OF ALASKA. . . Organized 1958
To promote the enjoyment of hiking, climbing, and exploration of the mountains;
Cultivation of mountain-climbing skills and techniques;
To teach and encourage mountain safety;
Maintenance of a trained group to be available for technical assistance to
    mountain rescue;
To assist in the prevention of waste and unnecessary destruction of the natural
    scene.

0 9 8 7 6
5 4 3 2

First edition, June 1972, revised June 1975
Second edition, December 1978, revised July 1981
Third edition, June 1985
© 1972, 1978 by The Mountaineers
© 1985 by Helen Nienhueser and Nancy Simmerman
All rights reserved

Published by The Mountaineers
306 Second Avenue West, Seattle, Washington 98119

Published simultaneously in Canada by Douglas & McIntyre Ltd.
1615 Venables Street, Vancouver, B.C. V5L 2H1

Manufactured in the United States of America
Designed by Marge Mueller
Layout by Constance Bollen
Cover photo: Hikers, Raven Glacier near Crow Pass—Trip 25
Frontispiece: Golden birch, Chugach National Forest (Simmerman photos)

Library of Congress Cataloging in Publication Data
Nienhueser, Helen.
    55 ways to the wilderness in Southcentral Alaska.

    Includes index.
    1. Hiking—Alaska—Guide-books. 2. Cross-country
skiing—Alaska—Guide-books. 3. Boats and boating—
Alaska—Guide-books. 4. Alaska—Description and travel
1981-   —Guide-books. I. Simmerman, Nancy. II. Title.
III. Title: Fifty-five ways to the wilderness in South-
central Alaska.
GV199.42.A4N54   1985   917.98'045   85-11503
ISBN 0-89886-106-3

Hans van der Laan
November 17, 1937 · April 2, 1971

To Hans

Who still lives in the hearts of his family and friends and who, through his part in the first edition of this book, shares with others his love of Alaska's mountains and valleys and his devotion to excellence.

"You cannot stay on the summit forever; you have to come down again . . . so why bother in the first place? Just this: what is above knows what is below, but what is below does not know what is above. One climbs, one sees. One descends, one sees no longer, but one has seen. There is an art of conducting oneself in the lower regions by the memory of what one saw higher up. When one can no longer see, one can at least still know."

From *Mount Analogue*, Rene Daumel, copyright 1959 by Pantheon Books, a Division of Random House, Inc.

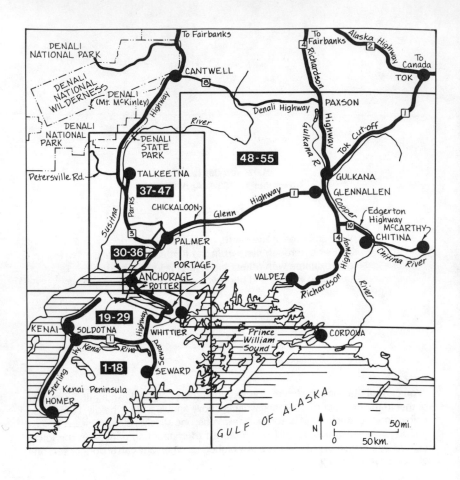

DENALI NATIONAL PARK

DENALI NATIONAL WILDERNESS

✕ DENALI (Mt. McKinley)

DENALI NATIONAL PARK

Petersville Rd.

To Fairbanks

CANTWELL 8

Parks Highway

River

✕ DENALI STATE PARK

TALKEETNA

Susitna

37-47

CHICKALOON

3

PALMER

30-36

PORTAGE

ANCHORAGE POTTER

Seward Hwy.

19-29

KENAI SOLDOTNA

Kenai River 1

WHITTIER

Sterling Hwy.

1-18

SEWARD

Kenai Peninsula

HOMER

48-55

Denali Highway

PAXSON

To Fairbanks 4

Richardson Highway

Alaska Highway 2

To Canada

TOK

1

Tok Cut-off

Gulkana R.

GULKANA

GLENNALLEN

Glenn Highway 1

Copper

Edgerton Highway

10

McCARTHY

4

CHITINA

Chitina River

Richardson Highway

Copper River

VALDEZ

Prince William Sound

CORDOVA

GULF OF ALASKA

N

0   50 mi.
0   50 km.

TABLE OF CONTENTS

Page

Preface: The Future of Alaska.... 9
Introduction: Hiking, Boating and
  Skiing in Southcentral Alaska .. 13
About This Book 27

KENAI PENINSULA
  Area Map 33
   1 Homer Beach Walk 34
   2 Swan Lake and Swanson River
     Canoe Routes 35
   3 Seven Lakes Trail 39
   4 Hidden Creek Trail/Kenai River
     Trail 41
   5 Skilak Lake Lookout 42
   6 Fuller Lakes 44
   7 Kenai River.............. 46
   8 Russian Lakes/Resurrection
     River Trail System 50
   9 Crescent Lake/Carter Lake .. 53
  10 Race Point 55
  11 Lost Lake 56
  12 Ptarmigan Lake 58
  13 Johnson Pass 60
  14 Resurrection Pass Trail
     System.................. 62
  15 Palmer Creek Lakes 64
  16 Hope Point 66
  17 Gull Rock 68
  18 Turnagain Pass Ski Tour 69

PORTAGE TO POTTER
  Area Map 73
  19 Byron Glacier View 74
  20 Bear Valley Ski Tour 75
  21 Portage Pass 77
  22 Alyeska Glacier View 79
  23 Winner Creek Trail 81
  24 Glacier Creek Ski Tour 83
  25 Crow Pass 86
  26 Bird Ridge 89
  27 Indian Valley 91
  28 Table Rock 93
  29 Old Johnson Trail 95

ANCHORAGE BOWL
  Area Map 101
  30 Rabbit Lake 102
  31 Flattop 103

Page

  32 The Ramp................105
  33 Williwaw Lakes 107
  34 Wolverine Peak 109
  35 Knoya and Tikishla Peaks ...111
  36 Rendezvous Peak 113

NORTH OF ANCHORAGE
  Area Maps.................116
  37 Eagle Lake 118
  38 The Perch 121
  39 Round Top and Black Tail
     Rocks..................122
  40 Thunder Bird Falls 124
  41 East Twin Pass...........127
  42 Bold Peak Valley 129
  43 Lazy Mountain and Matanuska
     Peak...................131
  44 Reed Lakes 133
  45 Hatcher Pass Ski Tour 135
  46 Craigie Creek 139
  47 Peters Hills..............141

CHICKALOON TO VALDEZ
  Area Map 144
  48 Hicks Creek/Chitna Pass 145
  49 Syncline Mountain.........148
  50 Gunsight Mountain in
     Winter 152
  51 Gulkana River 154
  52 Chitina Railroad Bed 157
  53 Kennecott Mines 159
  54 Worthington Glacier
     Overlook 161
  55 Mineral Creek Valley 163

APPENDIX
  Time of Year 166
  Length of Trip 167
  Canoe, Raft or Kayak Trips 168
  Good Trips for Children 169
  Trips Accessible from Public
     Transportation 170
  Information Sources..........171
  Organizations Concerned about
     Alaska's Future 172

INDEX 173

Lost Lake, July—Trip 11 (Simmerman photo)

Safety Considerations

Hiking in the backcountry entails unavoidable risk that every hiker assumes and must be aware of and respect. The fact that a trail is described in this book is not a representation that it will be safe for you. Trails vary greatly in difficulty and in the degree of conditioning and agility one needs to enjoy them safely. On some hikes routes may have changed or conditions may have deteriorated since the descriptions were written. Also, trail conditions can change even from day to day, owing to weather and other factors.

You can minimize your risks on the trail by being knowledgeable, prepared and alert. There are a number of good books and public courses on safety in the mountains, and you should take advantage of them to increase your knowledge. You should always be aware of your own limitations and of conditions existing when and where you are hiking. If conditions are dangerous, or if you are not prepared to deal with them safely, choose a different hike! It's better to have a wasted drive than to be the subject of a mountain rescue.

One element of the beauty, freedom and excitement of the wilderness is the presence of risks that do not confront us at home. When you hike you assume those risks. They can be met safely, but only if you exercise your own independent judgment and common sense.

The Publisher

PREFACE

THE FUTURE OF ALASKA

Why have we written this book? We have known and loved these mountains and valleys as wilderness and have found a special joy in walking here in solitude. We question our part in hastening a change by writing this book. Then why write it? Partly because we too were once newcomers here, once looked longingly at the mountains but didn't know how to get there. So we know the need for a guide.

But more important, Alaska needs your help, whether you are a resident or a visitor. Alaska does indeed hold America's last great wilderness. If our book leads you into Alaska's mountains, and if you come to love them as we do, you too can help to keep them as they are.

What is so important about Alaska? It is a symbol of wilderness, of freedom, of a way of life that is now only history in most of the United States. There was a whole-someness, a directness, a satisfaction in that life, lived close to the land, that is miss-ing from the lives of most Americans today. But because Alaska is there, and because Alaska still equals wilderness, there is hope. Hope that the values which made that way of life good may be rescued and made part of life again. Hope for each individual that he or she may someday experience Alaska's wilderness firsthand.

What are the values of wilderness? Among the most important are simplicity and directness. In today's America we are divorced from our primary needs. Someone else produces our food, erects our shelter, and protects us from nature's harsher elements. When we live in the wilderness, even for a weekend backpacking trip, we grapple once again with some of life's basic challenges, and we are dependent on ourselves alone for the solutions.

Wilderness is also beauty, peace, harmony, silence. A source of strength. The op-portunity, not to conquer nature, but to test oneself against the elements and to gain mastery over oneself. The opportunity to know ourselves and others away from the distractions of civilization. And more: aliveness, spontaneity, affirma-tion—qualities that make life more than mere existence. The farther we go from wilderness, the dimmer these values become. Without wilderness as a source of renewal, how long can we sustain them?

The existence of wilderness in the world is enough. Not everyone need go there. For many the dream will suffice. Wilderness remains a symbol for those who do not go, a direct source of renewal for those who do. Directly or indirectly, the lives of all will be enriched because wilderness exists.

What are the Chances?

Much of Alaska is still real wilderness regardless of whether the land is in or out of a park or whether it is owned by the federal or state government or a native cor-poration. When one flies over this land, one is struck by how small human impact has been. What are the chances of preserving that wilderness quality? That depends on the public. Change has come rapidly to Alaska since the discovery of oil at Prudhoe Bay in the late sixties. Along with oil development, major steps have been taken to protect Alaska's wild places. But by themselves, these steps are not enough. Public vigilance is still necessary to maintain Alaska's wilderness.

Many Alaskans feel strongly and sincerely that they have the right to see their state develop as other states have and that each individual should have the oppor-tunity to profit from the development. This is the frontier philosophy, a strong American tradition. There has been, however, a change in attitudes in Alaska in the past fifteen years. The conservation movement is now well established in Alaska. Although conservation and preservation are bad words to some, many others believe that times have changed, that there is no more wilderness beyond Alaska, and that the state's development must not and need not follow the pattern of other states. Although these changing attitudes bring real hope, the frontier philosophy is still strong.

Alaska became a state in 1959. During the first ten years of statehood, it did little to protect its lands. Then, in the early seventies, the legislature created Chugach, Denali, Kachemak Bay, and Chilkat state parks, along with various recreation areas and game refuges. In 1978, it created the Wood-Tikchik State Park (north of Dillingham). More recently, in 1983, a state marine park system was established.

In 1980 Congress passed what has been hailed by some as one of the greatest conservation acts of the century, the Alaska National Interest Lands Act. This act placed approximately 100 million acres of federal lands in national parks, pre-

Ridge walking, July—Trip 15 (Simmerman photo)

serves, and wildlife refuges. Large and representative samples of Alaska's wilderness and of its great and varied landscape were included.

More Remains to be Done

Important steps have been taken to protect Alaska's wild places, but more remains to be done. The protection promised federal lands by the national interest lands legislation could be negated by overdevelopment, overmanagement, and overregulation. Perhaps the greatest challenge lies on state lands, where the pressures for development are most intense and where there is the least protection. It remains important that the public recognize the value of wild places and work to protect them.

Now that large areas of Alaska are in federal parks and refuges, the questions to be answered are how to manage them and how much to manage them. Ideally, the more remote areas would be left essentially as they are with virtually no management except that which is necessary to protect them. The only way this will work is to avoid overpromoting these areas. If they are overpromoted, use of the areas will increase, and more intensive management will become necessary. Exploration of the unknown, the sense of mystery, risk taking, self-reliance, and the freedom to go where and when one chooses are vital parts of the wilderness experience. Too much information and too much management will destroy these opportunities. To be sure, there should be human use of these areas—but that use should be limited to those who care enough to work to find out where to go. This is self-limiting use—a much more acceptable kind of limitation than a permit system.

At the same time traditional uses of these areas must be allowed to continue. The existence of a subsistence-oriented lifestyle and of the native culture is an important part of Alaska's unique character. Hunting by local people in these areas is necessary in order to allow their lifestyles to continue. Access by small plane is necessary to allow use of many of the areas. However, while airplane access is essential, airplanes, too, could diminish the wilderness experience if unrestricted. There should be some valleys where the sound of an airplane is seldom heard.

To balance the areas left wild, some areas should be developed to accommodate heavier visitor use. The most appropriate areas for recreational development are the state parks, the national forest lands, and the national parks and refuges closest to population centers. Care must be taken to keep development harmonious with the natural areas and to limit and confine motorized uses.

The challenge on state lands is enormous. These include the public lands most accessible to Alaskans, and the limitless recreational opportunities they provide is what brought many people to Alaska in the first place. These are also the lands that grow timber, harbor minerals, and are desirable for private ownership. Striking the optimum balance among these uses is the challenge. Some areas—such as Hatcher Pass, the Talkeetna Mountains, Keystone Canyon, the Tazlina Lake area, and a number of the state's rivers—need special protection to ensure their continued availability for public use and the continued presence of wildlife. The national interest lands are generally remote from population centers and not readily accessible; thus they do not meet the need of Alaskans for weekend recreation. Some areas on state lands, such as those mentioned, are necessary to meet this need.

In other areas, the challenge is to allow some private uses without foreclosing existing recreational opportunities or lessening the quality of the recreational experience. A careful balance between public and private uses must be achieved. Scales tipped in favor of private uses could lead to a no-trespassing sign on every other tree, as is now the situation in many parts of the lower 48 states. This would mean the end of the wild and free Alaska most people came to enjoy, where one could camp and hike and hunt and fish almost anywhere.

U.S. Forest Service Resurrection River cabin (Nienhueser photo)

This book brings you directions for 55 ways to the wilderness—or perhaps to the edge of the wilderness. It is our hope that this book will serve to introduce you to Alaska's wild places and that you will go on from these trips to find your own ways to the wilderness. And that you also will take time out from your trips to let government decision-makers know that Alaska must remain a symbol of wilderness. A list of conservation organizations that can give you additional information on these issues can be found in the Appendix.

Helen Nienhueser
revised March 1985

INTRODUCTION

HIKING, BOATING, AND SKIING IN SOUTHCENTRAL ALASKA

This book is a guide to routes and trails that lead the hiker, boater, and skier to some of Southcentral Alaska's finest wild and beautiful back country. Hiking in Alaska is different from hiking in the more developed parts of the United States— we have few maintained trails. Fortunately many of the nicest places to go are above timberline where no trails are needed; walking is easy and pleasant on firm, dry tundra. The trick, especially in Southcentral Alaska, with its proliferation of brushy alder and willow, is getting above brushline.

55 Ways to the Wilderness in Southcentral Alaska describes numerous access routes to high country, making the best use of existing trails. As the population of the state grows, more trails are being built and maintained. In this book we've tried to create a pleasant balance among different kinds of trips—some through woodlands, some across tundra, a few float trips, and several winter trips for playing in the snow.

The book also offers trips for all skill levels. The novice who has never before ventured out of the city will enjoy starting with Trips 1, 19, 36, 38 and 40. The bulk of the book describes good solid trips of such beauty and variety that many of us like to redo them every few years. Some of the descriptions offer longer routes, for example Trips 48 and 51. These lead far from the road system, require a minimum of 3-5 days, and assume that the traveler can successfully plan and execute an extended wilderness trip.

Alternate routes and destinations are given in most of the trip descriptions. When all are tallied, this book could be more accurately titled *135 Ways to the Wilderness in Southcentral Alaska*. We suspect that many experienced Alaskan hikers will find new trips here. Though each trip is field-checked every few years, conditions may differ from those described here. Signs are erected or fall down; maintenance on routes improves or is discontinued. When possible, corrections are incorporated in new printings.

Getting There

Often just getting to the trailhead is an interesting excursion in itself. "Outsiders" are amazed at the types of roads that are labeled "highways" in Alaska. Nearly all are just two lanes wide, but most are paved. A few of the access roads are neither maintained nor marked. Each trip description gives specific information.

Because Alaskan roads and highways may be poorly marked, mileages are used for reference. Highways and primary side roads have mileposts every mile (more or less). Thus, if a trailhead is located between mileposts 35 and 36, we estimate the distance from the lower milepost, e.g. mile 35.3, Glenn Highway. If important mileposts were not standing, car odometers were used to estimate the mileage. Odometers were also used on side roads. Due to odometer differences, tire size and reference point, our distances may differ slightly from yours, but you'll be close to the trailhead and should find it with ease.

Travelers find it helpful to understand the state's system for numbering mileposts on Alaska's highways. Glenn Highway (Alaska Route 1) and Parks Highway (Route 3) mileposts begin in Anchorage. Richardson Highway (Route 4) mileposts begin in Valdez. Seward Highway (Routes 1 and 9) and Sterling Highway (Route 1) mileposts start in Seward and coincide for the first 37 miles. Edgerton Highway (Route 10) mileposts begin at the Richardson Highway.

Straightening and rerouting highways has created inconsistencies in the milepost system, with some posts closer than 1 mile, others 1.5 miles apart. Our figures are estimated from the nearest standing post.

When a road does not receive public maintenance, its condition varies greatly from year to year, with no guarantee it will be driveable. We have noted which roads might present problems. If you have doubts about whether your car can make it, don't try. Residents have become weary of pulling people out of mudholes and getting a tow truck yourself may take hours and be very expensive. Furthermore, driving on a soft, muddy road tears it up, which is unfair to local residents, who may maintain it themselves.

Following trail descriptions may also present a problem if trails are not marked or maintained. In such instances you are likely to wonder whether you are on the right trail, despite directions and maps. On roads and trails alike learn to trust your instincts and keep your sense of humor if you take the wrong fork. Retrace your steps and start again. Several hikes described here follow unmarked trails and roads that were created and are maintained only by public and animal use. Such unofficial routes can change annually.

A word of cheer for those who prefer paved roads and marked trails—we have some! Most are on the Kenai Peninsula and in Chugach State Park near Anchorage.

Boarding the Whittier Shuttle at Portage—Trip 21 (Simmerman photo)

Picking the time of year when each trip is "best" is sometimes difficult. The disappearance of the snow pack varies from year to year, but we've tried to choose representative dates. After a winter of heavier-than-normal snowfall, expect trails to open at least two weeks later than indicated. May is a tricky month in Alaska. At the lower elevations summer has arrived, but above 3000 feet winter weather dominates. For trips to high elevations take winter equipment. An easy climb in summer may call for a rope under winter conditions.

Hiking is usually good through September everywhere in Southcentral Alaska; below 3000 feet, trails may be snow-free well into October. In areas of light snowfall, trips near sea level often may be walked throughout the winter.

Where to Get More Information

Many of the trips described here are in the Kenai National Wildlife Refuge, Chugach National Forest or Chugach State Park. Insofar as possible, the trail descriptions are accurate, but up- to-date information can be obtained from appropriate state or federal land managers (addresses and phone numbers in the Appendix).

Each agency has its own regulations. In the Kenai National Wildlife Refuge and the Chugach National Forest, fire building and camping are unrestricted, although open campfires outside established campgrounds may be prohibited during times of high fire danger. Chugach State Park has few restrictions on camping, but permits campfires only in established campground firepits. Chugach State Park personnel encourage back-country travelers, for their own safety, to file a trip plan at the Park office or the Eagle River visitors' center.

The Forest Service maintains a number of cabins in the Chugach National Forest for public use. Reservations must be made well in advance through any of the U. S. Forest Service offices in Alaska. A user's fee is charged for both the cabins and national forest campgrounds. Unauthorized use of the cabins is a violation of both state and federal laws and regulations so be sure to have your permit with you.

Two publications helpful to hikers, campers and wilderness travelers in Alaska are *Alaska's Parklands* by Nancy Simmerman and *Mountaineering: The Freedom of the Hills*, edited by Ed Peters. Both books are published by The Mountaineers, Seattle, Washington. The volumes contain additional information about many of the topics discussed below.

Hiking with Children

Which hikes are good for children depends upon the child's age, ability, experience, and attitude. Experienced Alaskan hikers take their children along on almost all these trips, but some are certainly too long or difficult for the average child. Try your children on the easier hikes first. Babies can go almost anywhere in a kiddy pack; a 3-year-old should be able to manage several miles a day with an occasional piggyback ride; children of 5 and up can easily cover 4 to 5 miles a day and often more. Pick a trip that is interesting to the child, one that has a stream or lake to play in or rocks to climb on. A long, steep climb with no diversions is boring for children. Always carry water and favorite nibble foods, plus a small toy or two. See the Appendix for suggested trips.

Equipment

Walk a short distance from the road and you may be, for all practical considerations, in the wilderness. You must be self-sufficient, with proper clothing, food, and camping equipment and navigation aids. *Mountaineering: The Freedom of the Hills* lists ten essentials to be carried at all times: extra clothing, extra food, sunglasses, knife, matches, firestarter (e.g., candle), first aid kit (in Alaska, leave the snakebite kit home), flashlight (except in June and July), maps, and compass.

On a day trip, a knapsack is convenient for carrying extra clothing and lunch. A full backpack is appropriate for overnight hikes.

Hiking cross-country is easier and safer in sturdy boots with rubber lug soles. Most Alaskan trails have wet stretches; rain showers are often likely. To protect leather boots from moisture, waterproof them with one of the many preparations available. Reduce the chance of blisters by keeping boots pliable with boot grease, and always wear a pair of slippery lightweight synthetic or silk socks next to the skin under the heavier boot sock. Carry moleskin or, better, a roll of paper adhesive surgical tape (available at most drug stores), and cover any rub spots when you first notice them, not after a blister has formed.

Southcentral Alaska's mountains often experience a rain shower or two, even on the sunniest days. Many Alaskans routinely carry a lightweight rain poncho, a waterproof jacket, or a large plastic garbage bag for protection. Breathable waterproof raingear is good for general hiking, although only truly impermeable garments will protect against day after day of deluge.

Campfires

To avoid scarring Alaska's beautiful mountains, meadows, and trailsides, plan not to build campfires, especially in alpine areas, where plant life grows so slowly. Instead, carry a backpacking stove for cooking.

Alaska is subject to disastrous wild fires in dry years. Because of the slow decay rate, peat soil layers are particularly thick; these layers will burn and a campfire may spread under the surface. Throughout the 1969-70 winter at least 16 fires smouldered underground.

If you insist on having a campfire, please observe the following guidelines. First, to avoid creating new scars, build it at the site of a previous fire. Second, build it only on bare mineral soil (gravel or dirt); if a nonburnable soil is not available, don't build a fire. Third, to conserve living vegetation use only dead trees or brush for fuel. Be sure to have plenty of water to extinguish the fire, and, before leaving, make certain every spark is out. The infallible test is to touch the ashes carefully with bare hands. Also check the underside of any partially burned logs. Before leaving, thoroughly wet the surrounding area as well. Do not throw burning logs into a river or stream to quench them. A large forest fire was started on the Kenai Peninsula by just such a floating firebrand when it lodged against shore downriver.

Litter

All garbage and litter should be carried home. Burying garbage is not acceptable because animals will usually dig it up. In addition, the odor invites bears to investigate the campsite, endangering subsequent campers. If you have a campfire, burn paper, wet garbage and cans, then retrieve unburned items and take them with you in a plastic bag. The volume and weight will be surprisingly small.

Take care to bathe, wash dishes or clothes, and perform toilet functions all well away from streams and lakes. Use biodegradable soap and pour out the used water far enough away from natural water sources that it can sink into the soil rather than run off. Never use soap or detergents of any kind in lakes and streams.

Dispose of feces by burying them 6-8 inches deep and replacing the topsoil or tundra mat so the area will revegetate. Digging a new hole for each use is better for nature's decomposition system than creating a large community hole. Bury used toilet paper or carry it in a plastic bag until it can be burned; do not leave it on the surface of the ground. Burn used tampons or, if that is not possible, bury them immediately and never near camp.

Drinking Water

It's sad but true—drinking from Alaska's lakes and streams may be dangerous. Hikers who drink water contaminated with the microorganism *Giardia lamblia* may contract the painful and incapacitating illness commonly known as "beaver fever." Giardia are carried in mammal feces, including those of humans and dogs. Water in

Chugach State Park Visitors' Center at Eagle River (Simmerman photo)

and below beaver ponds is particularly suspect. Giardia cysts survive best in cold water and could possibly be found in any surface water. Bringing water to a boil will destroy the cysts. If other contaminating organisms might be present, boil it for at least 20 minutes. Treating water with tetraglycine hydroperiodide tablets is also effective. The tablets lose their potency when exposed to air, so replace them yearly. To remove giardia by filtration, the system must have a pore size of less than two micrometers.

Mosquitoes

Though generally not as much of a problem in Southcentral Alaska as in the Interior, mosquitoes are annoying to many people. Everyone should carry repellent during the summer, and those who are particularly sensitive should carry head nets.

Plants

Although Alaska is free of poison ivy and poison oak, it does have a few plants to be avoided. These include stinging nettle, devil's club, poison water hemlock, baneberry, and poisonous mushrooms. The Cooperative Extension Service (address in the Appendix) sells the useful booklets, *Wild Edible and Poisonous Plants of Alaska* and *Know Alaska's Mushrooms*. Other books on Alaska's plants and mushrooms are available at local bookstores.

Stream Crossings

A few of the hikes involve crossing potentially hazardous streams. To cross safely: (1) Look for the widest part of the stream, where the water will be the shallowest and least swift. (2) Wear boots to ensure good footing, first removing your socks to keep them dry. On the other side, put your socks back on; they will make walking comfortable even though your boots are wet. Running shoes can be used for crossings, but in really fast, deep streams, they do not protect your feet as well as boots. (3) Undo the waist strap of your pack so you can slip it off quickly should you fall. (4) Put your camera in a waterproof sack inside the pack. Its strap around your shoulders may make it impossible to remove your pack quickly. (5) For very swift water, use a rope to belay each person. (6) Use a stick or ice axe to probe for safe footing and to provide additional support. In swifter streams such as Eagle River, hold hands for stability. (7) Point toes downstream and walk diagonally, with the current. (8) Cross glacial streams in early summer or early morning, when water levels are likely to be lower. (9) Lightweight or small people should add rocks to their backpacks for more weight, thereby providing more secure footing.

A large braided stream may be crossed more easily if you take advantage of its natural flow pattern. Scout the river to find an area with many channels. Cross from the upstream end of one gravel island to the upstream end of the next. There the water is shallower and slower, due to gravel deposition. Just below such areas the water is swifter and deeper. The downstream end of a gravel island where channels converge may hide a deep turbulent hole or areas of soft sand.

Hypothermia

Cold weather is never far away in Alaska, even in midsummer. Hikers, boaters, and skiers should always travel with extra warm clothing and high-calorie snack foods. Excessive loss of body heat produces hypothermia—often called "exposure"—in which the body's metabolic and physiological processes are slowed. Death can result if body heat continues to be lost.

Cold weather, wetness (from rain or perspiration), wind, and fatigue or poor conditioning can impose a stress on the cardiovascular system. Whenever the body can no longer meet its heat and energy needs, hypothermia begins. For example, falling into cold water or just being wet at 50° F can lead to hypothermia.

Watch for the symptoms of hypothermia: a feeling of being chilled; uncontrollable, continued fits of shivering; vague, slow, slurred speech; memory lapses; incoherence; fumbling hands; frequent stumbling; drowsiness; and apparent exhaustion.

The victim often refuses to admit that anything is wrong, so members of the party must insist that treatment begin immediately. To avoid further loss of body heat, help the victim put on additional clothing and find shelter from wind. Body heat can be restored in cases of mild hypothermia by exercising, drinking warm liquids, and eating high-calorie foods.

When the body temperature nears 90° F, symptoms of severe hypothermia appear: shivering stops; the victim cannot walk without assistance and shows poor judgment, often leaving the parka unzipped and forgetting to wear cap or mittens. Eventually the victim may lose consciousness. Just before this happens, the victim may feel extremely warm and remove all clothing or crawl out of a sleeping bag.

Field treatment of severe hypothermia is often not successful. The central organs of a severely hypothermic person must be rewarmed before blood begins to recirculate through the arms and legs. If cold blood from the extremities reaches the heart before that organ is adequately rewarmed, ventricular fibrillation, an abnormal heart rhythm, commonly occurs and death follows.

Ventricular fibrillation can also be triggered by moving or jarring a severely hypo-

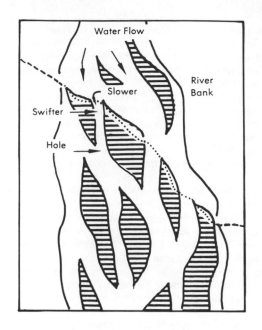

A braided stream showing gravel islands and a suggested route for crossing the stream.

thermic person. Arrange for evacuation by helicopter if the victim can reach proper medical facilities within 6 hours. Before making trips to remote areas, read the section about hypothermia in *Medicine for Mountaineering*, Third Edition, by James Wilkerson, M.D. and published by The Mountaineers in 1985. Dr. Wilkerson notes that a severely hypothermic person may not have a detectable heart beat, yet still be alive. Always rewarm a hypothermia victim before assuming that death has occurred.

Moose and Bears

One of the nicest events on an outing is seeing wildlife. Most sightings are occasions for photos and opportunities to observe the habits of Alaska's fascinating animals. Moose and bears, however, must be treated with distant respect. Experienced Alaskans recommend against taking an unleashed dog into the wilds; the dog may run after a moose or bear and end up being chased right back to its master.

Most moose will normally move away or ignore a hiker or skier. However, cow moose are fiercely protective of their calves and can be quite dangerous. Expect a cow to be nearby whenever you see a calf. Stopping to take a picture is not a good idea.

Bears, either black or brown (grizzly), can be dangerous and unpredictable, but most will not attack humans without provocation. Given sufficient warning and an avenue for retreat, most bears will head away from humans. Hikers should warn bears by making noise. This is especially important in deep brush, where it is possible to surprise a bear. Sing loudly, tie bells to your pack, waist or boots, shake pebbles in a can or metal canteen, beat on a pot with a spoon, blow on a noise maker. Don't whistle—you might sound like a marmot, a choice food. At night use a flashlight.

Constantly be alert for bear sign (bear trails, tracks, droppings, or diggings) and watch for the animal itself. If you spot a distant bear, avoid an encounter by changing your route or by sitting quietly until it has left the area. If you smell well-rotted fish or meat, you may be dangerously near a bear's food cache. Leave quietly and quickly.

Set up camp away from bear trails and salmon streams. If bear sign is abundant, reduce food odors by cooking dinner in one place, then continuing another half hour before camping in another. Do not keep food in your tent at night. Cache it in a tree or, if no trees are available, well away from the campsite. Keep all food well wrapped in plastic bags and do not carry especially odoriferous foods such as bacon or peanut butter. Mothballs in small net bags attached to the outside of food caches discourage animal raiders. Never feed bears, foxes, wolves, or wolverines. In Alaska it is illegal to do so either intentionally or by leaving food within reach.

Before going to bed, wash your hands and face carefully and brush your teeth to remove food odors. Do not use scented deodorants, perfumes or skin creams. Menstruating women should consider not camping in areas known to contain large populations of bears.

If, despite trying to avoid bears, you meet one, what should you do? Attempt to get out of sight, giving the bear plenty of room to avoid an encounter with you. If the bear has seen you, DO NOT RUN; it may decide to give chase, and you cannot outrun a bear. Instead, walk slowly backwards, facing the bear and talking sternly much as you would to a menacing large dog. If the animal continues to approach, drop your pack, jacket, anything to distract it and to give you more time to get out of sight.

Bears sometimes threaten with a charge, but veer away at the last moment. Stand your ground and increase your apparent size by waving your arms, jacket or poncho. Bears are not accustomed to creatures that do not run and may prefer not to investigate further.

If, despite your efforts, the bear seems certain to attack, drop to the ground and "play dead." Curl into a fetal position, put your hands over the back of your neck, and make no noise. Bears, like cats, are often not interested in a "lifeless" animal. Remain motionless until the bear is out of sight and well away from the area.

When traveling in bear country, carry something to protect yourself. Many Alaskans routinely carry guns; if you choose to do so, learn to handle it responsibly and to shoot accurately. If you are unable or prefer not to shoot, carry something else to discourage an inquisitive bear. Noise makers (firecrackers, shriek alarms, spoons on cooking pots) help, but more effective is spray from cans of insect repellent, paint, WD-40, or dog repellent. Mace and tear gas are designed for humans and do not work well against animals. The common highway flare used by motorists has also discouraged bears. In tents, campgrounds, cabins and other restricted or populated situations where use of firearms would be dangerous, plan to use one of the alternatives.

For a short description of bears' body language and other information, pick up a pamphlet entitled "The bears and you, or how to become a bear-wise sourdough in ten minutes," by Dave Hardy and Dave Kellyhouse (available in most parks and refuge visitors' centers in Alaska).

Boating

With few exceptions, Alaskan waters are very cold. The Kenai River drains fjord-like Kenai Lake, a natural reservoir of glacier runoff. Gulkana River, although not a glacial stream, originates in the foothills of the Alaska Range. Paxson Lake, the river's headwaters, remains ice-covered until mid-June, guaranteeing a chilly start.

A plunge into such cold water can create serious problems. Whenever a capsize is possible, dress warmly regardless of air temperature and have plenty of extra dry, warm clothes handy in a waterproof bag. Know how to treat hypothermia and give cardiopulmonary resuscitation (CPR). Many boaters wear wet suits for thermal protection and added buoyancy. Always wear a life jacket.

Be sure your boat will float even when full of water. Lash all gear securely. Inspect from shore any rapids before you float them; never attempt white water unless you

Gulkana River below canyon rapids, August—Trip 51 (John Ireton photo)

have considered all possible consequences of a capsize. If you do capsize, stay with the boat and work it to shore to ensure that your survival equipment is not lost.

The following river-classification system, employing the International White Water Scale, has been used in this book:

WW1 (Class I) Easy. Moving water with small regular waves, riffles and sandbanks. Some maneuvering is required.

WW2 (Class II) Medium. Rapids with numerous waves up to 3 feet and wide, obvious clear channels. Some maneuvering is required.

WW3 (Class III) Difficult. Rapids with numerous high, irregular waves capable of swamping an open canoe. A splash cover is necessary for open canoes and kayaks. Narrow passages require complex maneuvering. Scouting the route from shore is recommended.

WW4 (Class IV) Very difficult. Rapids with turbulent waters, rocks and dangerous eddies. Constricted passages require powerful, precise maneuvering and inspection of the route is necessary. This water is normally too difficult for experts in open canoes. Boaters in covered canoes and kayaks should be able to Eskimo-roll.

River ratings can change with water levels, some rapids becoming more difficult, some becoming easier. The rating of the upper Gulkana River, which lies far from

Glacier Creek canyon, January—Trip 24 (Simmerman photo)

the highway, has been increased due to the difficulty of rescue. Be particularly careful when help is far away. The presence of sweepers and snags increases the danger and may or may not be reflected in the river's rating.

Winter and Early Spring Trips

Special clothing and equipment are necessary for cold weather and winter travel. Carry severe-weather mittens, as well as a lighter-weight pair for traveling, extra wool socks, polypropylene long johns under wool pants or skiers' insulated warm-up pants, warm hat, and face mask. Polypropylene and wool fabrics are warmer, even when wet, than cotton. Gaitors, worn over pants bottoms and boot tops, keep the snow out. To avoid condensation, clothing should not be vaporproof. If you might encounter wet snow or rain, conditions that are all too common near salt-water, take breathable waterproof parka and pants.

Midwinter trips require additional equipment. A thick parka, down- or polyester-filled, with windproof hood, and insulated pants are recommended for day trips and mandatory on overnights. Many loosely fitting layers of clothing are warmest, with polypropylene underwear next to the skin.

Ski tourers should wear either insulated overboots over regular ski touring boots or a special double boot. Take mukluks or down- or synthetic-fiber-filled slippers (to wear under the overboots) for in-camp use on overnights.

In wet snow, snowshoers will be better off with insulated rubber "bunny" boots, waterproof shoepacs with a change of felt liners in the backpack, or hiking boots with insulated waterproof overboots. For cold snow (below 15° F), canvas or fur mukluks or bunny boots are good. Check the surplus and sporting goods stores for footgear. Snowshoes will travel up and downhill more easily if the frame is wrapped with heavy synthetic cord to provide greater traction. The toe of the boot should be able to move freely in the toe opening.

Sturdy but lightweight telemark touring skis with metal edges are ideal for explor-ing Southcentral Alaska's snow-covered mountains. Boots should be flexible but provide ankle support. Bindings must allow the heel to lift. Some downhill bindings can be used with an attachment that allows a free heel, but the units are heavy. Browse at ski shops and refer to books on winter equipment and travel for more detailed information. Careful waxing or the use of "no-wax" skis make climbing skins unnecessary except on steep slopes. 'No-wax" skis are excellent for the changing snow conditions found on spring ski tours.

Ski touring near Kenai River Trail, March—Trip 4 (Simmerman photo)

Frostbite

At low temperatures, particularly on windy days, be alert for frostbite, the damage resulting from the freezing of body tissues. Hands, feet, face and ears are normally the first to show the characteristic white patches. Wind chill speeds freezing, as does direct contact with metals and other highly conductive materials. When dexterity is important, wear thin "thermal" gloves to handle cameras, ski bindings, camping equipment, and the like.

Make a habit of checking each other's faces and ears frequently and train yourself to note the presence of sensation in your hands and feet. If feeling disappears, especially after a period of pain from the cold, immediately check for frostbite. A severely frostbitten extremity will be hard to the touch, without the softness of normal tissue.

Treatment of frostbite is complicated. To prevent permanent damage to tissues or joints, it must be done correctly. Understand the prevention and first aid treatment of frostbite before camping in the winter or making trips at low temperatures. An excellent source of information is *Mountaineering First Aid: A Guide to Accident Response and First Aid Care,* Third Edition, by Martha J. Lentz, Steven C. Macdonald, and Jan D. Carline, published by The Mountaineers in 1985.

"Frost nip," in which the surface of the skin shows white frozen patches while the underlying tissue feels normally soft, is the first stage of frostbite and should be treated immediately. Hold a warm hand over a frost-nipped nose, ear, or cheek to return the flesh to a healthy pink. Nipped fingers or toes can be warmed in an armpit or on a brave companion's stomach. Never rub a frost-nipped or frostbitten area with anything, especially snow.

A person with one area of frostbite may be hypothermic, so treat accordingly and check for further frostbite. Do not rewarm a severely frostbitten appendage in the field. Walking or skiing on a frozen foot does far less damage than traveling on rewarmed tissue. Get medical help as soon as possible.

Avalanches

If you travel through snow-covered mountains by foot, skis, snowshoes, dogsled, snowmobile, or automobile, know about avalanches. Avalanche deaths have increased in recent years in Southcentral Alaska as more people head to the hills for recreation.

Educate yourself and have a safe trip. Take an avalanche awareness course, an evening or weekend well spent. Contact the Alaska Avalanche School office (address and phone number in the Appendix) for the current schedule. Classes are held in Anchorage, Fairbanks, Juneau, on the Kenai Peninsula, and at Hatcher and Thompson passes. Meanwhile, study thoroughly *The ABC of Avalanche Safety,* Second Edition, by Edward R. LaChapelle, published by The Mountaineers. Before you go into the back country, find out about the current avalanche conditions by calling the Avalanche and Mountain Weather Forecast Recording (phone number in the Appendix).

Predicting which snow-covered slope will likely slide and which won't is a complex science and well beyond the scope of this book. Avalanches are most common on slopes of 30 to 45 degrees, the pitch most attractive to skiers. Be particularly careful on treeless slopes, during and after snowfalls, and after wind has transported snow from one area to another. Long periods of very cold weather can create an unstable snowpack as well. Before making a winter trip, discuss the safety of your route with a person trained in avalanche awareness.

Each member of a party venturing into hazardous areas should wear an avalanche-victim locator beacon and be trained in its use. Avalanche cords, once popular to lead searchers to a victim, are far less effective. Each person should also

Typical avalanche path down timbered mountainside. Upper mountain below ridge top (starting zone), blaze (track and runout zone), and nearby trees should be considered potentially hazardous in winter and spring. Although timbered slopes define avalanche zones, be alert for similar zones in treeless areas. Clearings to the right are natural. (Simmerman photo)

carry a shovel and something with which to probe the snow. Several brands of ski poles will convert to avalanche probes.

Being caught in an avalanche is a terrifying experience. You must fight for your life! Yell to attract your companion's attention, and try to get out of the avalanche to safety. If that fails, discard poles, and skis if possible, and swim vigorously to stay on the surface. As the snow slows, make an extra effort to reach the surface and thrust an arm upward. Rescuers will find you much faster if even a finger shows above the snow. If you cannot dig yourself free, relax to conserve oxygen. To calm yourself, meditate. Do not fight unconsciousness; your body needs less oxygen in that state.

If your companion is caught in an avalanche, note where the person was last seen. Before entering the avalanche path, check to be sure no further avalanching is likely. Place one member of your party in a safe spot to watch for additional slides, and establish an escape route for all searchers should another slide occur. Make a quick visual search of the area below the spot the victim was last seen.

If the party is not equipped with locator beacons, search in the most likely places. Leave the victim's discarded equipment in place to help localize the search area. Work in silence, listening for muffled cries from the victim. Probe the snow with ski

*Avalanche rescue beacon practice during avalanche awareness course
(Simmerman photo)*

poles, skis, tree branches, anything. In particular, check areas where the snow has accumulated—above trees or rocks, at the foot of the slide or the outside of a turn. Don't endanger your own lives through hypothermia, exhaustion or avalanche hazard, but be aware that the life of your companion depends upon your actions. If you find your companion, give CPR if necessary and treat for hypothermia. Search at least two hours before giving up.

Don't let fear of frostbite or avalanches deter you from enjoying the thrill and beauty of Alaska's winters. For many of us, snow time is an eagerly awaited part of the year, a time when rivers and swamps cease to be barriers and become highways to exciting new country that is inaccessible in summer. Be aware of the potential hazards and have a safe trip.

An Invitation

We hope you enjoy using this book as much as we have enjoyed preparing it. Exploring this magnificent land and compiling the information for you has brought to us a deep appreciation for all that Alaska represents. We ask that you treat the land with respect and teach others to do so as well. Do your part to preserve this heritage of unequalled wilderness by supporting efforts dedicated to this end. Conservation and recreation groups have formed in nearly every Alaskan community. Get involved!

Nancy Simmerman
revised March 1985

ABOUT THIS BOOK

The trips described are arranged geographically, from Homer to Valdez. The arrangement features trips on the Kenai Peninsula first, then works its way up the Seward Highway to the Anchorage Bowl. The "North of Anchorage" section extends from Eagle River through the western Talkeetna Mountains to low foothills just south of Denali (Mt. McKinley). The last section of the book explores the vast area defined by the Matanuska Valley, Glennallen, the Wrangell Mountains and Valdez.

Each trip description includes highway directions to the trailhead, trail notes, and other information pertinent to your enjoyment of the trip. Hiking times given have proven to be a good estimate for the steady but leisurely traveler who stops to enjoy the view, have a snack, and take a few pictures. Those hiking faster or slower will be able to adjust personal time estimates after just a few trips.

The stated elevation gain for each trip is cumulative and indicates how strenuous each trip might be. Often a traverse requires less climbing if started from a specific trailhead. Elevation at key points is given throughout the text. Trail distances are usually given to the nearest tenth of a mile. When a stated distance is less precise, fractions are used, for example 2½ miles.

The maps accompanying the descriptions give important information of interest to the hiker, skier or boater, but they should not be used for travel. Instead, use the book's maps to locate each trail on the U.S. Geological Survey (USGS) topographical maps listed with each description. The combination of the two types of maps will give you far more information than either map separately. Carry and know how to use USGS maps; without their information, you could become lost within a short distance of a road. Topographical maps show you what lies ahead on the trail and help you to plan routes and side trips. Never travel the wilderness without USGS maps. Finally, true north and magnetic north (as read from a compass) differ significantly in Alaska. Be sure you know how to correct for the difference. Addresses of USGS map sales offices are listed in the Appendix. A guide to symbols used on the USGS topographic maps is also available from the sales office.

Lazy day in camp, July (Simmerman photo)

LEGEND FOR MAPS IN THIS BOOK

Start of Trip   ●

Trails   **= = = =**

Route (when no trail exists, generally
above timberline)   • • • • • • •

Major Road   ━━━[1]━━━

Minor Road   ━━━━━

Abandoned Road   = = = = =

Railroad   ++++++++++++

Campground   ⛺

Point of Interest   ◇

Text Reference   ⟨1⟩

Building   ⌂

Town or Community   ●

Powerline   ı — — ı — — ı —

Land Unit Boundary   —··—··—··—

Stream and River

Lake or Body of Saltwater

Mountain Summit   ×6119'

Glacier

Engineer Lake, May—Trip 3 (Simmerman photo)

Hatcher Pass, February—Trip 45 (Simmerman photo)

Chugach Mountains from Pinochle Creek area, April—Trip 48 (Simmerman photo)

Hikers on Lost Lake Trail, July—Trip 11 (Simmerman photo)

Winter hiking on Kenai River Trail—Trip 4 (Nienhueser photo)

KENAI PENINSULA

1 Homer Beach Walk 34
2 Swan Lake and Swanson River
  Canoe Routes 35
3 Seven Lakes Trail 39
4 Hidden Creek Trail/Kenai River
  Trail 41
5 Skilak Lake Lookout 42
6 Fuller Lakes 44
7 Kenai River 46
8 Russian Lakes/Resurrection
  River Trail System 50

9 Crescent Lake/Carter Lake 53
10 Race Point 55
11 Lost Lake 56
12 Ptarmigan Lake 58
13 Johnson Pass 60
14 Resurrection Pass Trail System . 62
15 Palmer Creek Lakes 64
16 Hope Point 66
17 Gull Rock 68
18 Turnagain Pass Ski Tour 69

1 Homer Beach Walk

Round trip 4 miles or more
Hiking time 1–8 hours
High point sea level
Elevation gain none
Best anytime
USGS map Seldovia C5

A walk along the Homer beach takes you away from the bustle of the town and is a delightfully different Alaskan experience in summer or winter. Kachemak Bay, with its mountain backdrop, is one of Alaska's loveliest areas.

On the beach at low tide, look for starfish, many kinds of clam shells, mussels (alive and clinging to rocks in great profusion), whelk (neptune) shells, rocks covered with barnacles, sea urchins, snails, crabs, small shore birds, gulls, and kittiwakes. Coal and sometimes fossils can be found below the cliffs which border the beach. Waterfalls cascade to the beach; driftwood logs thrown up by storm waves provide ready benches and tables for picnics. Children of all ages, from toddlers to grandparents, will enjoy a walk in the brisk salt air.

At low tide hikers can wander along a broad sandy beach. High tides cover the sand, forcing hikers onto gravel and rocks near the base of the cliffs. Consult tide tables, available from most gas stations and banks, before setting out.

Pick a day with a reasonably low tide, start out before the low tide and return to Homer well before the tidal high. The highest tides come in all the way to the cliffs, a potential hazard. In some places the cliffs cannot be climbed, trapping the unwary. However, watch the hour and you'll have no problems. Wear rubber boots or well-greased hiking boots; many little inlets left behind by the retreating water must be crossed. Don't be caught as the tide pours back into these inlets, turning what were peninsulas into islands.

Homer is a charming seaside community at the end of the Sterling Highway, 226 miles south of Anchorage. To reach the beach, drive to the bottom of the Sterling Highway hill as it enters Homer. Opposite Pioneer Avenue, a gravel road, Olson Lane, bears right. Follow Olson Lane to its end and park on the small bluff overlooking the beach.

Wander the beach to the west as far as time permits. A good destination, an hour's walk away, is the rocky spit about 2 miles from Olson Lane. Extending far out into the water at low tide, it offers excellent beachcombing. Shortly after low tide this spit is covered by water, so plan your walk accordingly, allowing more time if you beachcomb en route.

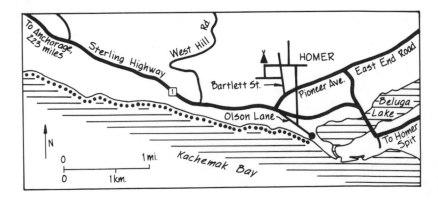

Beach at Homer, May (Nienhueser photo)

At very low tides good beachcombing is also available on the east side of the base of Homer Spit, at Mud Bay. Park on the spit road about a mile south of Kachemak Drive and walk out to the tidal flats. Camping is available in the city campgrounds on the hill above town (access from Bartlett Street) and on the spit (fees).

KENAI PENINSULA

2 Swan Lake and Swanson River Canoe Routes

Swan Lake: up to 60 miles
Allow 2 days to 1 week
River gradient 4 feet/mile
Best May–early October
USGS maps Kenai C2, C3

Swanson River: up to 80 miles
Allow 2 days to 1 week
River gradient 4 feet/mile
Best late May–early October
USGS maps Kenai D1, D2, D3, C2, C3
Kenai National Wildlife Refuge

This chain of lakes, streams, and rivers in the wooded northwestern Kenai Peninsula offers good safe canoeing and kayaking. Rough water is seldom a problem since the lakes are small and the rivers placid. Portages are short, well marked, and well cleared. Take 2 days or 2 weeks—many route variations are possible. More time means more fun exploring and fishing. A rich variety of water birds inhabit these waters, including many species of ducks and shore birds, loons, snipes, and swans. Anglers will find rainbow trout, Dolly Varden, steelhead trout, and land-locked salmon. Watch for moose, beavers, muskrats, and bears. In winter the canoe trails offer good ski touring.

The Swan Lake and Swanson River canoe routes are two separate systems. Both are reached from mile 83.5, Sterling Highway, 1.5 miles west of the Moose River bridge (136 miles south of Anchorage). (The Izaak Walton State Recreation Site beside the bridge is an exit for the Swan Lake Canoe Route.)

Gavia Lake, Swan Lake Canoe Route, June (Simmerman photo)

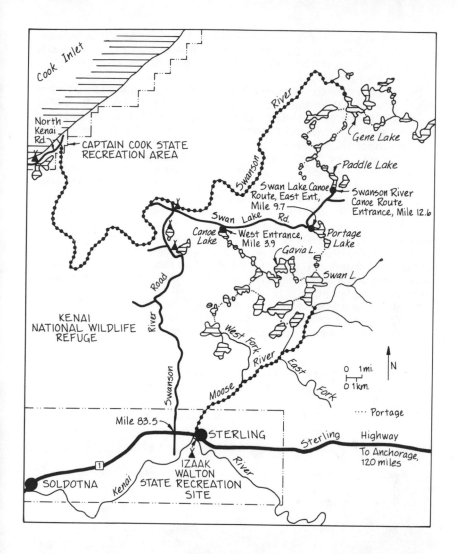

Turn north onto Swanson River Road (Robinson Loop Road). Expect no auto-mobile fuel beyond here. About 17 miles from the Sterling Highway is a junction with Swan Lake Road. Swanson River Road continues north 0.6 mile to the Swanson River and a campground. This is an exit for the Swanson River Canoe Route.

To reach the canoe route entrances, turn east onto Swan Lake Road. The Swan Lake Canoe Route lies south of the road; the Swanson River Canoe Route lies north of it.

The Swan Lake system has two entrances, the West Entrance at Canoe Lake, mile 3.9, Swan Lake Road, and the East Entrance at Portage Lake, mile 9.7. From either entrance the canoeist can reach Moose River and float it to the Sterling Highway bridge. This trip can be done in 2 long, hard days, but more time is recom-mended if you are not experienced at portaging boats and gear. Expect to reach Gavia Lake late the first day from either entrance. Plan to take several hours from there to Swan Lake and at least 6 hours to portage from Swan Lake to Moose River and float to the bridge. Camping along the Moose River during the first 1 ½ hours is poor. An easier 2-day trip is from one entrance to the other via Gavia Lake. Many other variations are possible.

The Swanson River Canoe Route entrance is at mile 12.6, Swan Lake Road, at Paddle Lake. From there explore various routes through the lakes or take a 2-day trip through a series of lakes and out Swanson River. To reach the river, head north to Gene Lake (1 day), then down Swanson River (12-14 hours) to the campground at the north end of Swanson River Road.

Another exit, about 12 hours farther, is near the mouth of the Swanson River at Captain Cook State Recreation Area. Highway access is from the city of Kenai. Drive to mile 38.5, North Kenai Road, and follow a side road south to reach the river.

Before planning to use this route, check the Swanson River water level with the Kenai National Wildlife Refuge office (address in the Appendix). Low water can make the first several miles of the river nearly impassable as it flows sluggishly through muskeg and dense masses of lily pads. The small stream connecting Gene Lake and Swanson River generally requires lining the boats and includes two short portages. A campsite can be found at the end of the second portage. Most campsites along the river are some distance back from the banks and require slogging through muskeg and marsh to reach them.

Good primitive campsites are available at most lakes in both systems. Build fires only on bare dirt in existing firepits, not on moss or peat, and be sure to pour lots of water on the fire and surrounding earth when you are finished. Campfires may be

Swanson River, Swanson River Canoe Route, May (Simmerman photo)

restricted in dry years. A 1969 fire in this area was caused by a careless camper. Cutting green trees is prohibited. Consider using a camping stove in this popular area, where firewood may be scarce. Wear rubber boots since lake shores and portages are often wet and boggy.

A brochure with maps showing the canoe routes is available from the refuge office. These maps are extremely helpful in locating connecting channels and portages, both of which are marked with small unobtrusive brown signs that are difficult to see from a distance.

Canoes can be rented in Anchorage, Soldotna and Sterling (addresses in the Appendix). Guided trips are available. The Swan Lake and Swanson River canoe routes are part of the National Trail and National Wilderness systems. No motorized off-road vehicles, including powerboats, snowmobiles, and aircraft, are permitted within the canoe route areas.

KENAI PENINSULA

3 Seven Lakes Trail

One way 5 miles
Hiking time 2–6 hours
High point 450 feet
Total elevation gain 150 feet
Best May–October
USGS maps Kenai B1, C1, C2
Kenai National Wildlife Refuge

A pleasant, easy walk for the whole family, the Seven Lakes Trail is especially enjoyable in early spring, when birds are returning to the Northland. The trail skirts lakes and winds through the Kenai burn of 1947, an area now growing up in young birch and spruce. Watch for common loons, red-necked grebes, surf scoters, greater scaups, arctic terns, swans, spruce grouse, pine grosbeaks, and many other species of birds. River otters often come out to play, so take a camera as well as binoculars and a bird book. Distant mountain vistas can be glimpsed across the lakes.

From mile 69, Sterling Highway (122 miles south of Anchorage), drive south to the Kelly Lake Campground via a 0.6-mile side road; the trailhead is marked (elevation 310 feet). The trail—easy walking over essentially flat terrain—first follows the shore of Kelly Lake, then, 1½ miles from the campground, skirts Hikers Lake.

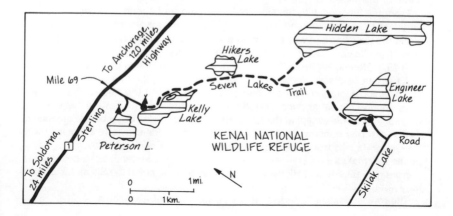

Engineer Lake, September (Simmerman photo)

About 2½ miles from Kelly Lake Campground (2 miles from Engineer Lake Campground), a 0.7-mile unmaintained side trail goes to the west end of Hidden Lake. At Hidden Lake, the side trail crosses a small stream in a stretch of unburned timber and continues a short distance to a pleasant, undeveloped campsite on the shore of the lake.

From the junction with the side trail, the main trail continues 2 miles south to Engineer Lake Campground (elevation 290 feet). There are wet, muddy sections along the way. The highway access to this trailhead is from Skilak Lake Road, 9.3 miles from its east end at mile 58, Sterling Highway, or 9 miles from the west end, mile 75.3, Sterling Highway. The trail begins at the north end of the campground.

A car can be placed ahead of time at the far end of the trail to avoid retracing steps, a consideration if small children are making the trip. Although good tent sites abound almost anywhere on the burn and firewood is plentiful, water is not generally available except at the lakes. Be sure to purify all water before drinking it. Kelly Lake has rainbow trout and Dolly Varden; Hidden Lake is especially well known for its lake trout as well as rainbows, Dolly Varden and salmon fry.

The trail makes a pleasant ski or snowshoe tour. For winter use, the best access is from mile 69, Sterling Highway, Kelly Lake access, since the Skilak Lake Road may not be plowed.

The trail is closed to off-road vehicles during snow-free months.

4 Hidden Creek Trail / Kenai River Trail

Hidden Creek Trail: round trip 3 miles
Hiking time 2–3 hours
High point 500 feet
Total elevation gain 0 feet in, 300 feet out
Best May–October
USGS map Kenai B1

Kenai River Trail: one way 6 miles
Hiking time 4–6 hours
High point 550 feet
Total elevation gain 250 feet northbound,
    550 feet southbound to Hidden Creek
    trailhead
Best May–October
Kenai National Wildlife Refuge
USGS map Kenai B1

A pleasant trip for the whole family, Hidden Creek Trail winds to the shore of Skilak Lake near the mouth of Hidden Creek. Watch for spruce grouse, moose, coyotes, wolves, and bears. At the lake, fish for rainbow and lake trout, Dolly Varden, silver and red salmon, and whitefish.

From mile 58, Sterling Highway (111 miles south of Anchorage), turn southwest onto Skilak Lake Road, marked by a sign for Skilak Lake Recreation Area. Drive 4.6 miles; the trailhead (elevation 500 feet) is marked. Park in the area provided across the road.

Hidden Creek Trail starts in the old Kenai burn of 1947, now well on its way to reforestation. Soon the trail drops into wet meadows and lush coniferous forest and crosses numerous streams. Logs have been laid across the trail to make walking

Skilak Lake near Hidden Creek, May (Simmerman photo)

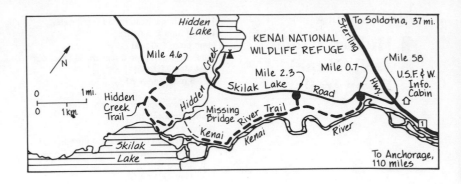

drier, but sections are still wet. Continue through a pleasant forest of evergreens and birch trees protecting a forest floor covering of moss, cranberry, crowberry and Labrador tea. The trail ends at the shore of Skilak Lake, where an endless supply of driftwood invites log-hopping and photographs. A short walk to the east along the lake shore is the mouth of Hidden Creek (elevation 205 feet). Pleasant mountain vistas grace the horizon. Campers should prepare for possible strong winds near the lake.

The Kenai River Trail, marked at the road, leaves Skilak Lake Road 0.7 mile from its junction with the Sterling Highway (elevation 300 feet). The trail heads down an old dirt road 0.2 mile to the river, then climbs uphill to the south and parallels the river downstream for about 6 miles. Another access to the trail is at mile 2.3 (elevation 700 feet).

The Kenai River Trail formerly connected with the Hidden Creek Trail and may again in the future. The bridge across Hidden Creek (about ¼ mile upstream from Skilak Lake) has washed out and may or may not be replaced. Without it, the creek is difficult to cross when water is high. If the bridge is not replaced, trails leading to it from each side will not be maintained and will become difficult to find. Check with the Kenai National Wildlife Refuge office (address in the Appendix) about the trail's current condition.

These trails and the Kenai River gravel bars are good ski or snowshoe trips, although in winter Skilak Lake Road may not be plowed. Wherever the river does not freeze over, watch for wintering bald eagles.

The trails are closed to off-road vehicles during snow-free months.

KENAI PENINSULA

5 Skilak Lake Lookout

Round trip 5 miles
Hiking time 3–5 hours
High point 1450 feet
Total elevation gain 750 feet
Best May–October
USGS map Kenai B1
Kenai National Wildlife Refuge

An easy-to-find trail through pleasant woods, with a lovely view at the end, this trip is good for children who can walk 5 miles or so. Watch for spruce grouse, moose and bears. Water is plentiful along the trail.

Skilak Lake from lookout, May (Simmerman photo)

At mile 58, Sterling Highway (111 miles south of Anchorage) turn southwest onto Skilak Lake Road (marked by a sign for Skilak Lake Recreation Area). Drive to mile 5.5; the trailhead (elevation 700 feet) is marked.

The Skilak Lake Lookout Trail leaves the south side of the road and climbs gently through pleasant woods. Streamlets cross the trail at more or less regular intervals, and a few spots in the trail may be wet. Occasional glimpses of Skilak Lake appear. Near the end, the trail climbs more steeply to a knob (elevation 1400 feet) from

43

Parka (arctic ground) squirrel cleaning up
(Simmerman photo)

which there is a fine panoramic view of Skilak Lake, the surrounding Kenai Mountains, Mt. Redoubt volcano to the west, and, to the northwest, Mt. Spurr and Mt. Gerdine. The view is well worth the trip.

There are no developed campsites here, but 6 public campgrounds are located along the Skilak Lake Road. In winter, if the road is plowed, this is a good snowshoe or ski trip.

The trail is closed to off-road vehicles during snow-free months.

KENAI PENINSULA

6 Fuller Lakes

Fuller Lake: round trip 6 miles
Hiking time 3–5 hours
High point 1725 feet
Elevation gain 1425 feet in, 35 feet out
Best June–October
USGS maps Kenai B1, C1

Skyline Trail traverse: one way 12 miles
Hiking time 8–12 hours
High point 3520 feet
Elevation gain 5370 feet westbound,
**   5410 feet eastbound**
USGS maps Kenai B1, C1
Mystery Creek Wilderness Unit, Kenai
**   National Wildlife Refuge**

Fuller Lake, a tempting jewel, lies just at timberline surrounded by scattered hemlocks, spruce, willow scrub and grassy meadows. Smaller Lower Fuller Lake, nestled just below timberline, is a good destination for families.

Hikers can make Fuller Lake their goal or continue up the ridge to the west for a panoramic view. Really energetic hikers may want to follow the Skyline Trail, which runs along the ridge top and finally descends to mile 61, Sterling Highway.

To reach the lakes, drive to mile 57.1, Sterling Highway (110 miles south of Anchorage), and park at a small pullout on the south side of the highway (elevation 300 feet).

The trailhead, an old road blocked by logs, is marked. Follow this old road north as it turns into a foot trail that climbs through forest and meadows and occasionally along a tiny stream. Look back frequently for views of Skilak Lake and the mountains to the southeast.

At Lower Fuller Lake cross the stream on a beaver dam. Continue along the left side of the lake and over a low pass to Fuller Lake, an ideal overnight spot. The lakes are actually in different drainages, Fuller Lake drains north into Mystery Creek, and Lower Fuller Lake, south into the Kenai River.

Ridges and knobs beckon from the lakes; brush presents little hindrance to exploration. The trail continues around the east side of Fuller Lake and then branches. The right branch continues a short distance north. The left branch leads up onto the ridge to become the Skyline Trail (not maintained).

To reach the Skyline Trail, cross the outlet of the lake and pick up the trail to the left of the small knob on the other side. Hiking the entire ridge traverse is a long, strenuous 1-day trip. A high meadow and spring at the western end offer a possible campsite, but otherwise snow banks provide the only water. Above brushline, the route is unmarked.

Lower Fuller Lake, October (Simmerman photo)

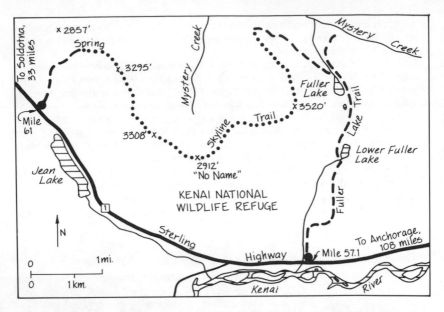

The Skyline Trail traverse terminates on the north side of the Sterling Highway just east of mile 61. The sign for the trailhead (elevation 450 feet) is, strangely, on the south side of the road. Park here at the gravel pit south of the highway; the trail begins on the north side of the guard rail. Taken from this end, the trail climbs very steeply and footing can be slippery on mossy and grassy slopes.

This area is included in the National Wilderness System. Off-road vehicles are not permitted during snow-free months.

KENAI PENINSULA

7 Kenai River

Kenai Lake to Upper Skilak Lake Camp-
ground: 19 river miles plus 6 lake miles
Allow 1 day
Gradient 14 feet/mile
Best May–October
USGS maps Seward B8, Kenai B1

Lower Skilak Lake Campground to Kenai:
45 miles
Allow 1 or 2 days
Gradient 4 feet/mile
Best May–October
USGS maps Kenai B2, B3, C2, C3, C4
Kenai River Special Management Area,
Alaska Division of Parks and Outdoor
Recreation

A good trip for rafters and for the intermediate or experienced canoeist or kayaker, the Kenai River offers just enough white water to be interesting. Caution is required because of swift, cold water and rapids.

After flowing from turquoise, mountain-rimmed Kenai Lake (elevation 436 feet), the river ends on the coastal flats of Cook Inlet, at the city of Kenai. The section above Skilak Lake, with its steeper gradient and undeveloped shoreline, is the more popular with floaters. Below Skilak Lake, the river is congested with powerboats and shoreline development. The shores abound with migrating and nesting birds. In autumn and early winter bald eagles, attracted by a late salmon run, perch on trees beside the river.

Eight entrances or exits for this trip make many variations possible. A good first trip, of medium difficulty (WW2), is from the bridge at Cooper Landing (1) to Jim's Landing (4), 13 river miles. This section has one set of WW3 (difficult) rapids at Schooner Bend (3); for the calmest water, travel against the right bank. (Classifications of river difficulty are described on page 21.)

For more experienced boaters, a longer 1-day trip, which includes the Kenai River canyon, goes from the bridge at Cooper Landing (1) to the Hidden Creek Trail (7), 19 miles, or to Upper Skilak Lake Campground (8), 6 miles farther along the lake shore. The canyon has 2 miles of WW3 rapids. Experience and splash covers for canoes and kayaks are necessary.

From Skilak Lake (9) (elevation 205 feet) to the city of Kenai (15), 45 river miles, the river is rated WW2 except for a single stretch of WW3 at Naptowne Rapids (11).

Boats may be portaged or lined around all rapids except those in the Kenai River canyon. Skilak Lake is subject to high winds, which swiftly whip up large waves and can therefore be dangerous. A number of lives have been lost when boats have overturned. Always stay close to shore.

Major points of interest along the way are: **(1) entrance, Kenai River bridge at Cooper Landing,** mile 47.8, Sterling Highway, 101 road miles south of Anchorage; a short side road leads to the river; 25 river miles to Upper Skilak Lake Campground, 76 river miles to the boat ramp at the city of Kenai's Cunningham Park; **(2) entrance-exit, bridge, mile 53, Sterling Highway; (3) Schooner Bend rapids** (WW3) immediately after the bridge; **(4) exit-entrance, mile 0.1, Skilak Lake Road;** a short side road leads to Jim's Landing Campground and boat launch; **(5) Kenai River canyon,** 2 miles of WW3 rapids; **(6) Skilak Lake,** about 3 miles below the canyon; stay close to shore; **(7) exit, Hidden Creek Trail** (Trip 4) to Skilak Lake Road, 30 minutes away by foot; **(8) exit, Upper Skilak Lake Campground,** 6 water miles along the lake shore from the Kenai River; highway access, 10 road miles on Skilak Lake Road from mile 58, Sterling Highway; **(9) entrance, Lower Skilak Lake Campgound,** 6 miles by water from

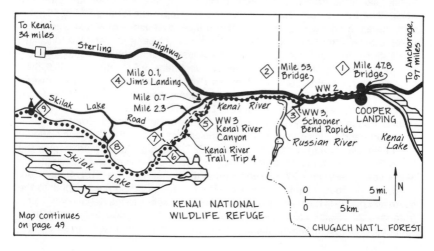

Map continues on page 49

Upper Kenai River, May (Simmerman photo)

upper campground; 45 river miles to the city of Kenai; highway access, 16 miles on Skilak Lake Road from mile 58, Sterling Highway; **(10) Skilak Lake outlet into the Kenai River,** 2 miles from lower campground; **(11) Naptowne Rapids** (WW3), 10 miles downstream from Skilak Lake; **(12) exit-entrance, confluence of Moose and Kenai rivers,** 3 miles after Naptowne Rapids; land on right bank at Izaak Walton State Recreation Site boat ramp, ⅛ mile up lazy Moose River; highway access, mile 82, Sterling Highway; **(13) exit-entrance, Kenai River bridge at Soldotna,** mile 95.9, Sterling Highway; **(14) tidal action influences river flow beginning halfway between Soldotna and Kenai; (15) exit, city of Kenai's Cunningham Park,** picnic site and boat launch; highway access is from mile 2.5, Beaver Loop Road.

Safety dictates that boaters inspect all white water before attempting it. The Schooner Bend rapids can be seen from the access road to the Chugach National Forest Russian River Campground at mile 52.7, Sterling Highway. To inspect the Kenai River canyon rapids, drive to mile 58, Sterling Highway and turn south on Skilak Lake Road. Drive 0.7 mile and park at the Kenai River Trail (Trip 4) trailhead. Follow an old road 0.2 mile to the Kenai River. The trail then heads uphill to the south and parallels the river downstream. Another access to the Kenai River Trail is from mile 2.3, Skilak Lake Road. When floating the river, double-check difficult spots by landing and walking the shoreline to determine the best route around ob-

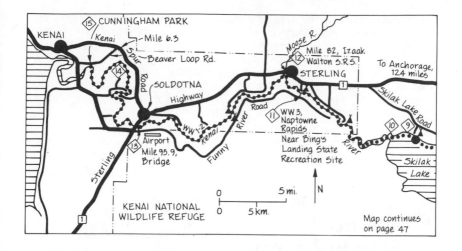

Map continues
on page 47

stacles. The difficulty of rapids will vary according to water level, some becoming more difficult at high water, others less difficult.

Boaters should always wear Coast Guard-approved flotation vests. Two or more boats should travel together, maintaining sufficient distance between them to allow complete freedom of route. Wear enough warm clothing or, better yet, wet suits, to protect against cold water in case of capsizing. The extreme cold of the water can cause rapid exhaustion and even loss of consciousness. Some of the route is not near a road and help is often far away.

The Kenai River has become an extremely popular waterway for anglers and power boaters as well as non-motorized boaters. In 1984 the river corridor became part of the Alaska Division of Parks' system. The Division of Parks and Outdoor

Upper Kenai River, September (Simmerman photo)

Recreation (address in the Appendix) manages the river to reduce conflicts between recreational users and to control development along the river. Park rangers patrol the river in summer. During the July and August red salmon runs, the waters near the confluence with the Russian River are the most intensively fished in the state, with anglers often standing shoulder to shoulder; avoid tangling with fishing lines as you float by. The river system also produces world-class king salmon weighing up to 90 pounds. Most of the river within the Kenai National Wildlife Refuge will continue to be managed by refuge personnel.

KENAI PENINSULA

8 Russian Lakes / Resurrection River Trail System

Lower Russian Lake: round trip 6 miles
Hiking time 3 hours
High point 800 feet
Total elevation gain 300 feet in, 300 feet out
Best May–October
USGS map Seward B8

Upper Russian Lake: round trip 24 miles
Allow 2 days
High point 700 feet
Total elevation gain 800 feet in, 600 feet out
Best May–October
USGS maps Seward B8, Kenai B1

Cooper Lake to Russian Lakes: one way 21 miles
Allow 2 days
High point 1450 feet
Total elevation gain 350 feet
Best June–October
USGS maps Seward B8, Kenai B1

Russian Lakes to Resurrection River: one way 31 miles
Allow 3–5 days
High point 1200 feet
Total elevation gain 1500 feet
Best June–October
USGS maps Seward A7, A8, B8, Kenai B1
Chugach National Forest

This trail system offers many possibilities including an afternoon hike from Russian River Campground to Lower Russian Lake; a weekend trip to Upper Russian Lake; an overnight from Cooper Lake to Russian River Campground; and a 3–5-day trip from either Russian or Cooper Lake trailhead to the Resurrection River trailhead near Seward. In combination with the Resurrection Pass Trail (Trip 14), a 7–10-day trip of 70 miles can be enjoyed. All options offer a beautiful forest walk with cascading clear streams, brilliant wildflowers, berries in season, moose, and bears. Glaciered mountains can be glimpsed through the trees along most of the trails. Fishing can be excellent in the Russian River, but check fishing regulations before trying it.

To reach the Russian River Campground trailhead, from mile 52.7, Sterling Highway (106 miles south of Anchorage), turn south onto a side road marked "Chugach National Forest Campground, Russian River." (Do not confuse it with the Kenai National Wildlife Refuge, Kenai-Russian River Campground at mile 55, Sterling Highway.) Follow the campground road 0.9 mile to a marked parking area for the Russian Lakes Trail (elevation 500 feet). During the salmon runs in July and August, the area is extremely crowded with anglers; fees are charged for parking, camping and fishing.

Resurrection River Trail, August (Nienhueser photo)

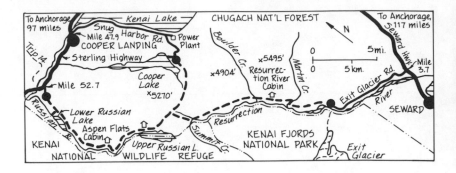

The hike to Lower Russian Lake (elevation 550 feet) is a nice 1-day family trip although the pretty woodland trail is somewhat marred by a mining road crisscrossing it. Occasional anglers' trails branch off the trail, but the main trail is marked. Shortly before Lower Russian Lake the trail crosses Rendezvous Creek on a bridge. To reach Lower Russian Lake, just before the bridge take a right-hand fork in the trail and parallel the creek to its confluence with Russian River. Follow this anglers' trail upstream ¼ mile to the lake or downstream ¼ mile to Russian River cascades. The anglers' trail can also be followed downstream to Russian River Campground.

To reach Upper Russian Lake (elevation 690 feet) follow the main trail across Rendezvous Creek and on to the south for another 9 miles. The Forest Service maintains two cabins, one at Aspen Flats, 9 miles from the trailhead, and one at Upper Russian Lake (boat available for those with reservations) at mile 12. Make reservations with a U.S. Forest Service office (addresses in the Appendix).

Another fine overnight hike is from Cooper Lake to the Russian River trailhead, a distance of 21 miles. The Cooper Lake trailhead (elevation 1300 feet) is 950 feet higher than the far end—it's downhill most of the way! To reach the Cooper Lake trailhead, from mile 47.9, Sterling Highway (101 miles from Anchorage), follow the Snug Harbor Road 11 miles southeast to a marked parking area. The 9-mile trail to Upper Russian Lake is a scenic walk through wooded mountain valleys.

A more strenuous hike is to the Resurrection River trailhead (elevation 400 feet) near Seward, from either the Russian River trailhead (31 miles) or the Cooper Lake trailhead (20 miles). The Resurrection River Trail leaves the Upper Russian Lake/ Cooper Lake Trail about 5 miles from the Cooper Lake trailhead or 16 miles from the Russian River trailhead and descends the Resurrection River drainage for 15 miles. The trail winds through thick forest with occasional glimpses of mountains or the river. The first creek south of Summit Creek has a good campsite, but, generally, good campsites are scarce. Occasional meadows offer possible campsites in dry weather. The Forest Service Resurrection River cabin is about 1½ miles down the trail south of Boulder Creek, near an unnamed creek. A word of caution: in August and September, the National Forest's largest concentration of brown (grizzly) bears feed upstream of the bridges over Boulder and Martin creeks.

To reach the Resurrection River trailhead by road, drive to mile 3.7, Seward Highway. Follow the Exit Glacier Road 7.5 miles to a parking area at the trailhead.

The entire system makes good ski trips in winter, but it is also used by snowmobilers. Be alert for slopes that could avalanche. (See "Avalanches," page 24.) The Snug Harbor Road is plowed in winter 8.5 miles to the Cooper Lake Power Plant on Kenai Lake. The other access roads are not plowed. The trail is closed to off-road vehicles from April 1 through November 30 and closed to horses from April 1 through June 30.

9 Crescent Lake/ Carter Lake

Via Crescent Creek: round trip 12.8 miles
Hiking time 5-8 hours
High point 1550 feet
Total elevation gain 960 feet in, 100 feet out
Best June-October
USGS maps Seward B7, C7, C8

Via Carter Lake: round trip 8 miles
Hiking time 3-5 hours
High point 1550 feet
Total elevation gain 1050 feet in,
   100 feet out
Best June-October
USGS maps Seward B7, C7
Chugach National Forest

Hike an excellent trail to a pretty lake near timberline. Make this a glorious September hike through the golds and reds of autumn. The trip is good for families with children, if reservations are made for overnight use of the U. S. Forest Service cabin located at the west end of Crescent Lake. A rowboat goes with the cabin, and fishing for grayling is good. The opposite (east) end of Crescent Lake can be reached via a shorter but steeper trail that goes first to Carter Lake. Unless the cabin is the main objective, the east end of the lake is a nice alternate trip. Six miles of steep,

Crescent Creek at Crescent Lake, September (Simmerman photo)

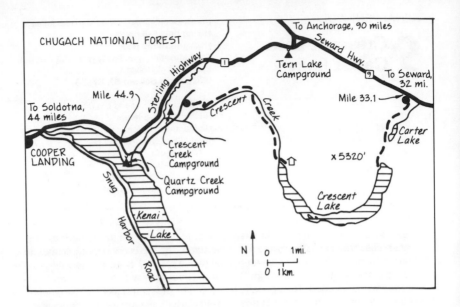

brushy slopes separate the ends of Crescent Lake, with no trail between them.

At mile 44.9, Sterling Highway, about 8 miles west of the junction of the Sterling and Seward highways and 98 miles south of Anchorage, turn south on a road marked "Quartz Creek Recreation Area." Follow this road 3.3 miles to the Crescent Creek trailhead (marked), 0.5 mile beyond the Crescent Creek Campground.

The Crescent Creek Trail starts directly across the road from the parking area (elevation 590 feet). The trail winds gently through birch-aspen woods along a tiny stream, climbs over a low ridge, and descends into Crescent Creek canyon. Follow the trail upstream, crossing the creek on a bridge, and continue upward, often on the hillside well above the creek. The trail now wanders through patches of woods and across avalanche-cleared swaths, finally emerging in a broad, open meadow dotted with trees. Cross Crescent Creek again on a bridge near the lake outlet (elevation 1454 feet). The cabin is a short distance along the lake shore beyond the bridge. Make cabin reservations through a U.S. Forest Service office (addresses in the Appendix). High country is easily accessible from here.

To reach Crescent Lake via Carter Lake, drive to mile 33.1, Seward Highway (94 miles south of Anchorage). The trail, an old jeep trail originally built as part of a now-discarded plan for access to a water resource, leaves from a parking area on the west side of the highway (elevation 500 feet). Cross the foot bridge at the trailhead and climb the switchbacks of this pleasant 2.3-mile-long trail to Carter Lake (elevation 1486 feet). A foot trail continues another mile around the west side of the lake and on to Crescent Lake. In winter this trail makes an excellent ski tour; skiers can continue across Crescent Lake to the cabin. Crescent Creek Trail is hazardous in winter due to avalanches. (See "Avalanches," page 24.)

Both ends of the lake have good campsites. Water is available, but the wood supply is primarily brush. Moose and bears may be spotted in summer; wolverines occasionally in winter. Crescent Creek Trail is closed to off-road vehicles and horses from April 1 through June 30 because of soft trail conditions. Carter Lake Trail is closed to off-road vehicles from April 1 through November 30 and closed to horses from April 1 through June 30.

KENAI PENINSULA

10 Race Point

Round trip 3 miles
Hiking time 44 minutes to 6 hours
High point 3022 feet
Total elevation gain 2900 feet
Best April–October
USGS map Seward A7

In 1915, the year the railroad from Seward led to the founding of Anchorage, a bet in Seward started a race still repeated every 4th of July. The runners in this mountain marathon start from the Seward town center, near sea level, climb to Race Point (elevation 3022 feet), at the end of the southeast ridge of Marathon Mountain, and return. The record is 43 minutes, 11 seconds, set in 1981 by Bill Spencer. Independence Day is the most exciting time to make the climb, whether you are in the race or not, but it is a good hike anytime during the summer.

Two trails climb to Race Point. The Hikers' Trail is extraordinarily steep, but the Runners' Trail is even steeper. Fortunately, the Hikers' Trail provides a spectacular view of Seward and Resurrection Bay, giving ready excuse for pause. The hiker may choose to go up the Hikers' Trail and down the Runners'; the two are within easy walking distance at their lower ends.

To reach the Hikers' Trail, find First Avenue in Seward, the street that runs along the base of Marathon Mountain. Drive to its intersection with Monroe Street. The extension of Monroe Street is a dirt road. Park here (elevation 200 feet).

Walk up this road, marked "Marathon Municipal Water Supply," to an abandoned building, then follow a foot trail steeply uphill through a rich forest of large hemlocks. Abruptly the forest ends, and alders take over. Here a jeep road climbs to the municipal dam. Go down this jeep road 10–20 paces, watching for a somewhat overgrown foot trail that continues upwards through alders and ferns. It may be marked with surveyor's tape. The trail is worth searching for since it is the most pleasant way up the mountainside. When you reach the ridge crest, note the spot

City of Seward and Resurrection Bay from Hikers' Trail, November (Simmerman photo)

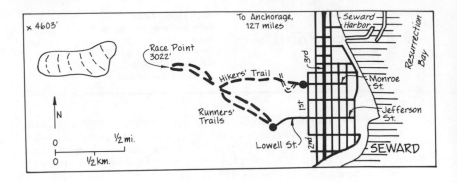

carefully if you will be returning on this trail; the Hikers' Trail is hard to find on the way down since it intersects the more traveled Runners' Trail.

Follow the ridge upward. The trail to the "summit" at 3022 feet becomes poorly defined on the rocky ridge. Unless you are a runner, sit awhile to enjoy the impressive view of Resurrection Bay and the glacier-streaked mountains beyond. Look for ptarmigan, parka squirrels, marmots, mountain goats, and Dall sheep.

The Runners' Trail is better known. Drive west on Jefferson Street into Lowell Creek canyon. (Jefferson becomes Lowell Street.) The trailhead, marked, is in a small gravel pit (elevation 300 feet) just beyond the water storage tanks. The first section of the trail is steepest, requiring the use of hand holds in spots. The runners ascend the ridge to the right of the gully and return in the scree of the gully.

Snow patches remain near the top well into July, but these can be easily avoided. The lower part of the Hikers' Trail is open early in the spring and still provides glorious views. The gully on the Runners' Trail has snow late into the summer and cliffs always—fun for the adventurous. Climbing the true summit of Marathon Mountain (elevation 4750 feet) requires experience and mountaineering gear.

KENAI PENINSULA

11 Lost Lake

Round trip 14 miles; traverse 15 miles
Hiking time 7–10 hours
High point 2000 feet
Total elevation gain 1900 feet; from
    Primrose Landing, 1600 feet
Best late June–September
USGS maps Seward A7, B7
Chugach National Forest

In July this is perhaps the most beautiful and photogenic trail the Kenai Peninsula has to offer. Climbing through a hemlock and spruce forest, the trail emerges above treeline on tundra and flowered meadows accented by stands of weathered, gnarled hemlocks. The area was at one time heavily glaciated; now brilliant blue lakes fill every depression, reflecting the snow-covered summits of surrounding mountains. Lost Lake, the largest, is forced into a strange shape by the topography. The area invites camping and exploring. Water is plentiful but firewood scarce, so take a cooking stove. A few small fish populate Lost Lake, and marmots abound in the nearby rock slides. The trail is good for family outings and ski or snowshoe trips.

Lost Lake, July (Simmerman photo)

The trailhead (elevation 100 feet) is at mile 5.1, Seward Highway (122 miles south of Anchorage). Park in the designated area west of the highway.

On foot, follow the marked trail, a logging road, until it becomes a well-defined foot path. After 1½ miles, a winter trail branches off to the right. Follow the left-hand path which winds through a pleasant forested canyon. Occasionally Resurrection Bay can be seen glistening in the distance. The latter part of the route is entirely above brushline. At about mile 6, the trail emerges on a glacier-scarred bedrock bench and, in another mile, reaches Lost Lake (elevation 1920 feet).

Salmonberries are ripe in August along the trail near mile 4. Some years snow may persist into July, making the portion above timberline hard to follow.

Climbing to the summit of Mt. Ascension (elevation 5710 feet) is a goal best left to mountaineers, who may need ice axes and crampons. However, scrambling partway up the steep lower slopes for a sweeping view is definitely recommended. A side trip, easy walking over firm tundra, around the southwest edge of the lake and up the valley to the west, brings a splendid view of the steep north side of Mt. Ascension. Look for mountain goats and bears. A cross-country hike from here to Cooper Lake is possible. (See Trip 8.)

To hike from Lost Lake via the Primrose Trail to Kenai Lake, head east to the lake's outlet, Lost Creek. Cross the creek on a bridge and follow the trail markers for 2½ miles along the east side of the lake and through alpine areas to the Primrose

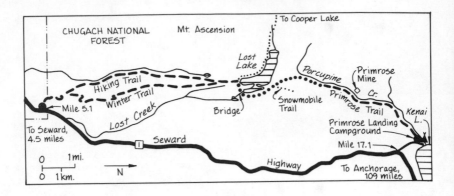

Trail. (The bridge across Lost Creek is generally snowfree from mid-June through August.) Primrose Landing Campground (elevation 450 feet) at Kenai Lake is about 6 miles away. North of the pass, on the east side of Porcupine Creek, find the trail on a ridge as it parallels the creek. Do not follow the orange markers for a winter trail, which leads into the forest east of the pass.

To find the Primrose trailhead by road, turn off the Seward Highway at mile 17.1 at a sign for Primrose Landing Campground. Drive about a mile to the road's end and continue to the farthest campground loop. The trailhead is marked.

The trail is closed to off-road vehicles from April 1 through November 30 and closed to horses from April 1 through June 30.

KENAI PENINSULA

12 Ptarmigan Lake

Round trip 7–15 miles
Hiking time 4–8 hours
High point 900 feet
Total elevation gain 450 feet in, 150 feet out
Best May–October
USGS maps Seward B6, B7
Chugach National Forest

A turquoise beauty, Ptarmigan Lake reflects the mountains that surround it. Two trails with magnificent views lead from the highway to join shortly before the lake; a 4-mile extension of the trail continues around the lake to the east end.

Entering by one trailhead and leaving by the other makes a nice loop trip; the trailheads are only a mile apart. When you return from Ptarmigan Lake, high grasses obscure the turnoff to the northern trail. Therefore the loop is best hiked beginning at the northern trailhead. Anglers will find grayling, salmon, Dolly Varden, and rainbow trout in Ptarmigan Creek, and grayling in Ptarmigan Lake.

To reach the northern trailhead, drive to mile 24.2, Seward Highway (103 miles south of Anchorage). Slightly north of the Trail River Campground entrance, a gravel road with a stop sign leads east. Follow this road across the tracks and park near the tracks (elevation 450 feet).

On foot continue east a short distance. The road passes a house and an old log cabin. Respect private property and do not litter. As the road turns right, near the cabin, the Ptarmigan Lake trail continues straight ahead. A Forest Service sign may

East end of Ptarmigan Lake, June (Simmerman photo)

mark the trailhead, but the trail is not well maintained, so signs may be down. Ptarmigan Lake is about 3 miles away. The first part of the trail follows an old mining-access road.

About a mile from the trailhead, just beyond the remains of a burned cabin in a clearing and a creek crossing, the trail turns right leaving the old road. Climbing a low, timbered ridge, it then contours along the mountainside at about 900 feet elevation, well above the valley floor. Look for glimpses of Ptarmigan and Kenai lakes. Soon this trail intersects the Ptarmigan Creek Trail, which originates at Ptarmigan Creek Campground. Continue straight ahead to Ptarmigan Lake (elevation 755 feet).

This is a good destination for picnicking or overnight camping. Or continue around the north shore of the lake about 4 miles to the eastern end, which also of-

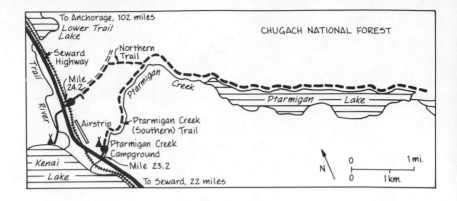

fers good campsites. Abundant driftwood lies on the beaches. Fallen trees and an eroded bank or two are minor obstacles along the north shore, but the trip is well worthwhile.

The southern trailhead (Ptarmigan Creek Trail) is located in the Ptarmigan Creek Campground (elevation 450 feet) at mile 23.2, Seward Highway. The scenic trail, 3½ miles long, follows the tumbling clear creek upstream, then turns away to climb through a quiet conifer forest to meet the northern trail.

Originally the route continued beyond Ptarmigan Lake into Paradise Valley, then followed the Snow River back to the railroad. That segment is now badly overgrown. The accesses to the Paradise Valley were built in the 1930s by the Civilian Conservation Corps.

Avalanche hazard precludes winter use of either trail beyond the first 1½ miles. Hikers arriving by light plane can land on the Lawing airstrip between the trailheads. The Ptarmigan Creek Trail is closed to off-road vehicles and horses from April 1 through June 30.

KENAI PENINSULA

13 Johnson Pass

Traverse 21 miles
Allow 2 days
High point 1500 feet
Total elevation gain 900 feet southbound,
   1000 feet northbound
Best June–September
USGS maps Seward C6, C7
Chugach National Forest

Between 1908 and 1910 the Alaska Road Commission constructed a trail for pack horses and dog teams through Johnson Pass en route to the gold fields of the Iditarod area. The first shipment of gold, over a half million dollars worth, left Iditarod in December 1911, taking 54 days to reach Seward. This hiking trail follows portions of that route; watch for traces of the old trail, abandoned cabins and ruins of wagons.

To reach the Granite Creek (northern) trailhead just south of Turnagain Pass, drive to mile 63.8, Seward Highway (63 miles south of Anchorage). A marked 0.4-mile side road leads south to a parking area (elevation 600 feet). The southern trailhead (elevation 500 feet) is at mile 32.7, Seward Highway, near Upper Trail Lake.

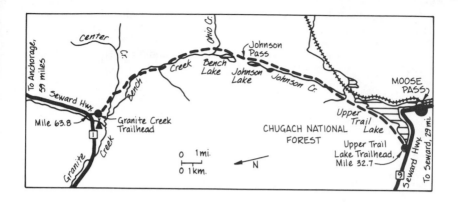

From the Granite Creek trailhead the route winds through open meadows and forest, crossing Center Creek (mile 2.2) and Bench Creek (mile 3.8) on bridges. Walking only as far as the bridges makes a pleasant day's outing. Beyond the second bridge the trail enters V-shaped Bench Creek valley and follows the creek to its source at Ohio Creek and Bench Lake.

After crossing Ohio Creek (mile 8.9), the trail follows the eastern shore of Bench Lake and climbs imperceptibly to Johnson Pass (mile 10; elevation 1500 feet). South of Johnson Lake, the trail parallels Johnson Creek but is above it in the woods. About 9 miles south of the pass, the trail emerges on the shore of Upper Trail Lake and follows the shore to the southern trailhead at mile 32.7, Seward Highway.

Good campsites can be found above timberline at Johnson Pass and below timberline at the south end of Johnson Lake (mile 11).

The Center Creek valley and the first 7 miles of trail from the southern trailhead make good ski trips, but stay well away from slopes that could avalanche. (See "Avalanches," page 24.) Due to severe avalanche hazard, winter travel through the

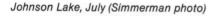
Johnson Lake, July (Simmerman photo)

pass between the Bench Creek bridge and mile 12, 2 miles south of Johnson Lake, is not recommended. The Center Creek drainage and the northern part of the trail as far as the Bench Creek bridge are closed to vehicles year-round. The entire trail is closed to off-road vehicles and horses from April 1 through June 30 because of soft trail conditions.

KENAI PENINSULA

14 Resurrection Pass Trail System

Up to 38.6 miles
Allow 2–7 days
High point 2600 feet
Total elevation gain 2100 feet southbound,
  2200 feet northbound
Best June–September
USGS maps Seward B8, C7, C8, D8
Chugach National Forest

Hikers wanting a long backpack trip on a good trail through the always-beautiful Alaskan mountains, will enjoy the Resurrection Pass trail system on the Kenai Peninsula. The most popular route, 38.6 miles long between the Hope trailhead and the Sterling Highway, is normally done in 3 days by sturdy hikers and in 5 or more days by families. There are 9 public-use cabins and fishing along the way. This route

Resurrection Pass from Summit Creek Trail access, July (Simmerman photo)

was one of the trails traveled in the late 1890s by gold seekers coming from Resurrection Bay to the gold fields near Hope.

Four alternate trips connect with this route to make an intriguing trail system: Hope trailhead to the Seward Highway via Devil's Pass or Summit Creek trails (about 31 miles); Devil's Pass or Summit Creek trailheads to the Sterling Highway (about 27 miles); Summit Creek trailhead to the Devil's Pass trailhead (about 20 miles); Hope, Summit Creek or Devil's Pass trailheads to the Exit Glacier Road near Seward via the Russian Lakes/Resurrection River trails (Trip 8), a distance of up to 70 miles. All trails except Summit Creek, an old miners' trail, are maintained.

To begin the hike at the Hope trailhead, drive to mile 56.3, Seward Highway (71 miles south of Anchorage). Turn north at the Hope Highway, drive to mile 16.1, then turn left onto Resurrection Creek Road and continue 4 miles to the trailhead (elevation 500 feet) at Resurrection Creek.

The cabins are well spaced for a 5-day trip, although families may prefer a longer trip using more cabins. Make cabin reservations with a U. S. Forest Service office (addresses in the Appendix) well in advance. For those unable or not wishing to use the cabins, campsites are easy to find.

The trail follows wooded Resurrection Creek valley to the creek's headwaters in the open tundra of Resurrection Pass, then down Juneau Creek valley, through forests and beside mountain lakes to the Sterling Highway. Points of interest (see map) are: (1) Caribou Creek cabin (mile 7.1 from the Hope trailhead); (2) Fox Creek cabin (mile 12.5); (3) East Creek cabin (mile 14.4); (4) Resurrection Pass (mile 19.3, elevation 2600 feet); (5) Summit Creek trail access (about mile 20); (6) Devil's Pass cabin and Devil's Pass trail junction (mile 21.4); (7) Swan Lake cabin (mile 25.8) and access to West Swan Lake cabin, fishing, boats available for renters at both cabins; (8) Juneau Lake cabin (mile 29.1), fishing, boat; (9) Romig cabin on Juneau Lake (mile 30), fishing, boat; (10) Trout Lake cabin via 0.5 mile side trail (mile 31.8), fishing, boat; (11) Juneau Creek Falls (mile 34.1). The trail terminates at mile 53.1, Sterling Highway (elevation 400 feet) just west of the Kenai River bridge.

The Devil's Pass Trail begins at John's Creek, mile 39.5, Seward Highway (elevation 1000 feet) and climbs to 2400-foot Devil's Pass. It joins the Resurrection Pass Trail at about the same elevation.

The Summit Creek Trail (sometimes referred to as the East Creek Trail) leaves the west side of the Seward Highway at mile 43.8. Park in a pullout on the east side of the highway (elevation 1350 feet). On foot, follow a rutted, eroding dirt road under a powerline to the ruins of mining buildings. Beyond, a foot path parallels Summit Creek, climbs over two passes (elevations 3450 feet and 3350 feet), then descends to Resurrection Pass (cumulative elevation gain 2850 feet). The east-bound Summit

63

Creek Trail is very difficult to locate from the Resurrection Pass Trail.

Watch for moose, Dall sheep, marmots, and brown (grizzly) bears. In late June and early July, wildflowers turn the tundra into a visual delight. No firewood is available at the pass.

A fine ski or snowshoe tour is from the Hope trailhead to the Sterling Highway, but prepare for blizzards in the pass and, in mid-winter, the possibility of below-zero temperatures. Devil's Pass and Summit Creek trails are not recommended due to severe avalanche hazard. (See "Avalanches," page 24.)

The Resurrection Pass and Devil's Pass trails are closed to off-road vehicles, including snowmobiles, from February 16 through November 30 and closed to horses from April 1 through June 30.

KENAI PENINSULA

15 Palmer Creek Lakes

Round trip 2 miles or more
Hiking time 1–4 hours
High point 2950 feet or more
Total elevation gain 750 feet or more
Best July–September
USGS map Seward D7
Chugach National Forest

High in the hills above the old mining community of Hope is the scenic valley of Palmer Creek. Here the tundra is punctuated by waterfalls and weathered hemlocks. Higher yet, a hanging valley cradles two alpine lakes. This is a delightful day trip for children and agile grandparents alike. The only sobering note is the last 5 miles of road—high, narrow, winding—but normally driveable in dry weather by most cars with sufficiently high clearance. The road is unsafe for large camper vehicles and trailers.

Gold was first discovered on Palmer Creek by George Palmer in 1894. A rush to the Turnagain gold fields took place in 1896. Two towns, Hope and Sunrise, grew out of the rush, and as many as 5000 people were reported living in the area in 1898. Palmer Creek was the site of early placer mining and, later, lode mining, beginning in 1911 with John Hirshey's Lucky Strike vein. Mining continued into the 1930s.

At mile 56.3, Seward Highway (71 miles south of Anchorage), turn north at the Hope Highway, drive to mile 16.1, then turn left onto Resurrection Creek Road. In 0.7

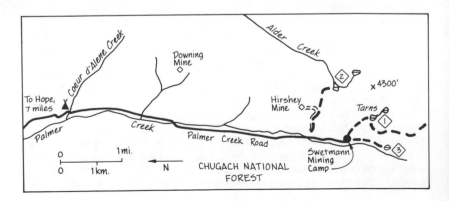

mile, continue straight ahead on Palmer Creek Road, following it about 12 miles to its end at the abandoned Swetmann mining camp. (The road is not maintained beyond the Coeur d'Alene Campground at mile 7.) Park near the old mine buildings.

The trail begins near the cabins (elevation 2200 feet), just north of the stream. A steep footpath climbs the hillside to the east and leads to a pretty hanging valley (1) with tarns (alpine lakes). Although steep, the trail is short, less than a mile in length, and passes a waterfall. A larger waterfall can be reached by cutting south across the hillside below the steepest part of the trail—a nice detour on the way back down. The tarns, nestled at 2950 feet, below sheer rock walls, are fine picnic spots. Hikers who enjoy rock scrambling will find many inviting ridges and small peaks in the area. A ridge particularly easy to climb is southwest of the tarns.

Another set of lakes (2) lies at about 3000 feet elevation at the head of Alder Creek, just over the ridge above the Hirshey mine.

Finally, families in particular may enjoy a gentle mile-long stroll up the valley from their parked cars to a small knob with a fine view. A tiny gemlike tarn (3) lies hidden behind the knob.

Camp at the Coeur d'Alene Campground or well away from the trails to minimize impact on the fragile tundra. Children will enjoy fishing for golden fin trout in the beaver ponds along Palmer Creek.

The mining buildings are private property and should be left alone. Because of the elevation and northern exposure, the road in this narrow valley usually cannot be driven until July, and even from then through August patches of snow and ice may remain along the stream and at the lakes.

Considerable avalanche danger makes this area hazardous for winter and spring use.

Tarn above Palmer Creek, September (Simmerman photo)

16 Hope Point

Round trip 5 miles
Hiking time 4–8 hours
High point 3708 feet
Total elevation gain 3630 feet
Best May–October
USGS map Seward D8
Chugach National Forest

Spectactular and very steep, the route to Hope Point offers impressive views of Turnagain Arm from a different angle than is usually available. The vista north across Turnagain Arm puts into perspective those familiar Chugach Mountains southeast of Anchorage. Take extra maps (Seward B7, Anchorage A7 and A8) to help locate favorite spots.

At mile 56.3, Seward Highway (71 miles south of Anchorage), turn north onto the 18-mile, scenic Hope Highway. Go around Hope, continuing another mile to the road's end at the Chugach National Forest Porcupine Campground. Park in the campground (elevation 80 feet).

Walk the campground road back toward the entrance sign to tiny Porcupine Creek. An unmarked foot trail follows the right- hand side of the stream, providing a lovely creekside walk beside water tumbling gently over mossy rocks. The first ⅓ mile meanders beside the stream under a canopy of large alders.

The trail then climbs the bluff to the right and continues steeply upward through forest. Soon the trees thin to a meadow parkland studded with evergreens. Climb at least to the first rocky outcropping (elevation 800 feet), far enough to get a view up the Resurrection River valley. The valley is particularly pretty in autumn, when the birch-aspen forest is a brilliant gold. Plan on taking about 15 minutes to stroll along the stream and another half hour to reach the outcropping. To this point the trip is suitable for young children. At the outcropping, you are essentially above timberline and only your physical condition limits you on the steep hike up the rest of the ridge to the summit of Hope Point (elevation 3708 feet). Expect no drinking water after Porcupine Creek.

Devil's club (Simmerman photo)

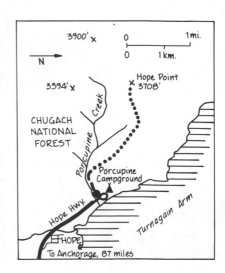

Turnagain Arm from ridge below Hope Point, October (Simmerman photo)

En route are sweeping views of Turnagain Arm, the mountains rimming it, Cook Inlet, and Fire Island. Note the speed of the tide as it flows in and out; watch for a tidal bore, the well-defined leading wave of an incoming tide. Grasses, mosses, crowberries, bearberries, caribou moss, and ground cedar cover the slopes between scrub hemlock and alder patches. Moose and bear droppings are abundant, so watch for the animals themselves.

From Hope Point the ridge to the south beckons for miles. Lack of water is the most limiting factor, although in early summer snow patches should be available for melting. Plan to spend as much time as possible in this alpine wonderland.

17 Gull Rock

Round trip 9 miles
Hiking time 5-7 hours
High point 700 feet
Total elevation gain 620 feet each way
Best May-October
USGS map Seward D8
Chugach National Forest, Kenai National
    Wildlife Refuge

To enjoy the smell and sound of the ocean, take this delightful walk to Gull Rock along the southwest side of Turnagain Arm. Watch for moose on land, beluga whales in the water, and bald eagles in the air. The views of the Arm and the mountains beyond are especially nice in spring and fall, when the trees bordering the trail have dropped their leaves. Hikers of any age will appreciate this gentle trail.

The trail is an old wagon road built in the late 1920s. It leaves the Hope area and parallels Turnagain Arm westward for 4½ miles. Although the trail is cleared of brush only to Gull Rock, the route connects with a tractor trail a few miles to the west, where a natural-gas pipeline from the Swanson River oil field crosses Turn-

Turnagain Arm from Gull Rock, November (Simmerman photo)

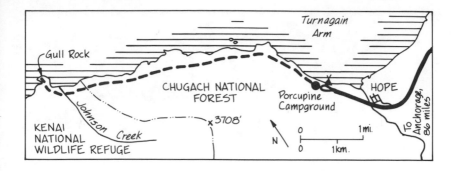

again Arm. The reminders of earlier days are fascinating: bits of old corduroy road-bed, the remains of a cabin and stable on Johnson Creek near the end of the trail, a mossy old bridge crossing the creek, the ruins of a sawmill.

To reach the trailhead, drive to mile 56.3, Seward Highway (71 miles south of Anchorage). Turn north onto the 18-mile Hope Highway and drive around Hope, continuing another mile to the road's end at the Porcupine Campground. The trailhead (elevation 80 feet) is at the far end of the campground.

Winding along the shoreline well above tidewater, the trail reaches an elevation of 700 feet before dropping back down to Gull Rock. The way is never steep. Breaks in the trees afford views of the Arm and shoreline. The variety of vegetation along the trail ranges from pleasant birch-aspen woods to alder-choked gullies, from stately hemlock forests carpeted by deep moss to a tundra-like area with tiny spruce, mosses, lichens, lingonberries, and saxifrages. At one point the trail crosses an avalanche gully so steep and straight that it looks like a suicidal bobsled run, ending in the tidewater of Turnagain Arm.

Beyond Johnson Creek, continue on the trail to the rocky promontory of Gull Rock (elevation 140 feet). Sit and listen to the turbulent water swirl around the rocks below as the tides flow in and out. On the other side of Turnagain Arm, a tiny stream of cars flows by on the Seward Highway near McHugh Creek Picnic Area.

Water can be found along the trail, but few good camping spots are available. Fires should be built only on bare dirt or rock, not on peat or moss. The best camping is at Porcupine Campground. The trail is closed to off-road vehicles and horses from April 1 through June 30.

KENAI PENINSULA

18 Turnagain Pass Ski Tour

Round trip 6 miles
Skiing time 3–5 hours
High point 2200 feet
Total elevation gain 1200 feet
Best November–April
USGS map Seward D6
Chugach National Forest

For a delightful ski or snowshoe tour, try Turnagain Pass, which generally has lots of deep snow and is one of the few places closed to snowmobiles. Winter was meant to be like this—snow crystals glinting in the sunlight or huge flakes falling

Ski touring on Center Ridge, March (Simmerman photo)

softly through giant hemlock trees, towering snowy peaks, and, best of all, the rich silence of the mountains.

To reach the trailhead (elevation about 1000 feet), drive the Seward Highway to mile 68, at the Turnagain Pass winter sports area, 59 miles south of Anchorage. The U.S. Forest Service has designated the west side of the highway for snowmobiles and other motorized winter vehicles and the east side for nonmotorized winter sports. Access to the parking area for skiers and snowshoers, on the east side of the highway, is 0.2 mile south of the snowmobilers' pullout (located west of the highway). Outhouses are provided at both parking areas.

On skis, head toward the gentle, forested slope to the southeast, crossing Tincan Creek en route, and look for orange diamond-shaped markers indicating the trail. The route winds slowly uphill through conifer forest and natural clearings. Snow hangs heavily on the trees, creating imaginary giants and monsters. After about ½ mile, the route swings to the base of the ridge separating Tincan and Lyon creeks and climbs a small treeless bowl to the ridge crest. Trail markers end here. (Do not continue along the base of the ridge below open snowy slopes; the slopes could avalanche from either side. See "Avalanches," page 24.)

Even a short trip winding through these snow-laden trees is an excursion into the best Alaska's winters have to offer. Timberline, at about 2000 feet elevation and 1½ miles from the parking area, makes a good destination for a short day. If time allows, continue on the crest of this rolling moraine, traversing the north side of the higher knobs and following the ridge crest until it begins to climb to the mountain peak. Jagged white mountain ridges rise all around making this an unforgettable winter experience.

In midwinter the sun seldom reaches the moraine, so dress warmly. Fortunately, wind is unusual here. Except for the slopes above tree line, the route is avalanche-free, as are the hemlock-studded ski-touring slopes northeast of the parking area at the base of Tincan Ridge. Before venturing out in the snowy Alaskan mountains, take one of the many interesting avalanche seminars offered to the public each winter. Skiers have been killed by avalanches on nearby mountain slopes.

The east side of the Seward Highway from Bench Creek to Ingram Creek, including Turnagain Pass, is closed to off-road vehicles year-round.

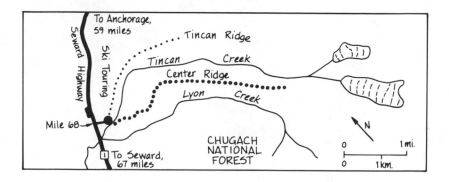

Center Ridge ski trail, February (Simmerman photo)

Iceberg in Portage Lake, March—Trip 19 (Simmerman photo)

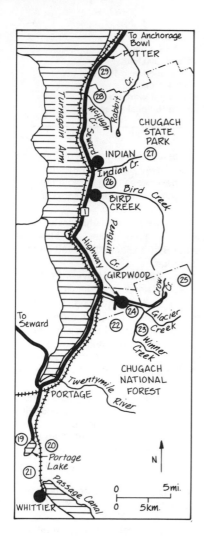

PORTAGE TO POTTER

19 Byron Glacier View 74
20 Bear Valley Ski Tour 75
21 Portage Pass 77
22 Alyeska Glacier View 79
23 Winner Creek Trail 81
24 Glacier Creek Ski Tour 83
25 Crow Pass 86
26 Bird Ridge 89
27 Indian Valley 91
28 Table Rock 93
29 Old Johnson Trail 95

19 Byron Glacier View

Round trip 2 miles
Hiking time 1 hour
High point 300 feet
Total elevation gain 100 feet
Best May–October
USGS map Seward D5
Chugach National Forest

This wide and smooth trail is a delightful walk for families with small children, for Aunt Minnie, and for spry great-grandmother. An easy hike with essentially no climbing, the trip is exciting for those who have never seen rugged mountain and glacier terrain up close. Bring a picnic lunch and relax in the heart of snow-and-ice country.

From Portage at mile 78.8, Seward Highway (48 miles south of Anchorage), drive the 5.7-mile paved road east to Portage Lake. At the Portage Glacier Lodge take the right-hand fork and continue bearing right to the Byron Glacier trailhead parking area (elevation 200 feet), about a mile from the lodge.

On foot, follow the trail south to a fine view of snow-capped Byron Peak and Glacier. The alders along the pathway make wonderful horses for young children to ride. Byron Creek, along the last half of the trail, is handy for throwing stones into; the vast quantities of smooth stones build into tottering towers and fortresses.

About a mile from the parking area, a large permanent cone of snow is a remnant of avalanches that swept across the valley in previous winters; it is great for snow fights or sliding. Recently, this snow cone has opened sizeable crevasses and should be approached with caution. Unwary hikers could fall into the ice cave and Byron Creek.

Look on the snow cone for ice worms—black, less than an inch long, and slender as a thread. Yes, they really do exist! In the evening and on cool days, these tiny annelids, relatives of the earthworm, eat pollen and algae on the surface of the snow. Since they can live only at temperatures near the freezing point of water, ice worms must escape the heat of the sun or the sub-freezing cold of winter. They do this by sliding into the snow or ice between crystal faces, an amazing little niche in the ecosystem.

Traveling onto the glacier itself is for experienced, properly equipped mountaineers only. Do not venture into ice caves or near towering ice faces, both of which can collapse.

Although summer temperatures are cooler than in Anchorage, the Byron valley is

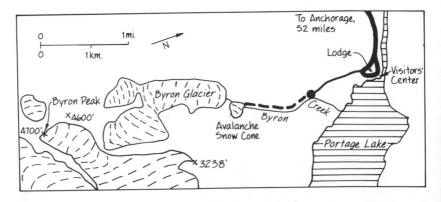

Byron Peak and Glacier from avalanche snow cone area, June (Simmerman photo)

protected from the icy winds that blow across Portage Lake. Here the sun is warm. For camping, use one of the excellent Forest Service campgrounds you passed on the road coming in. Considerable avalanche danger makes this valley unsafe during winter and spring. (See "Avalanches," page 24.) Byron valley and Portage Lake are closed to off-road vehicles year-round and to horses from April 1 to June 30.

PORTAGE TO POTTER

20 Bear Valley Ski Tour

Round trip 6 miles
Skiing time 4 hours
High point 200 feet
Total elevation gain 50 feet
Best December–April
USGS map Seward D5
Chugach National Forest

Bear Valley, a tranquil winter paradise, seems far away from the bustle of the road system, but it actually lies just minutes from Alaska's most popular visitor attraction—Portage Lake and Glacier. Bear Valley's accessibility makes this an ideal wilderness ski or snowshoe trip for those short mid-winter days.

Placer Creek tributary, December (Simmerman photo)

From Portage, at mile 78.8, Seward Highway (48 miles south of Anchorage), drive the 5.7-mile paved road east to the Portage Glacier Visitors' Center parking area, beside Portage Lake (elevation 150 feet). Be sure the ice is strong enough for safe travel; it should be at least 4 inches thick.

On skis or snowshoes, head east across Portage Lake, being careful to avoid potentially thin ice near the lake's outlet into Portage River and at the mouth of Placer Creek. Stay at least 100 feet from icebergs frozen into the lake. They often roll in the winter, breaking up the ice around them. If pressure ridges are present, watch for open water.

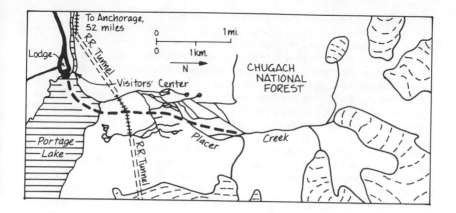

Swing left into Bear Valley, the valley that enters Portage Lake from the north, and cross the railroad tracks near the center. Stay well away from the mountainsides to avoid avalanche danger. (See "Avalanches," page 24.) Although the width of the valley makes the center generally safe for touring, it is best avoided entirely during periods of extreme avalanche hazard.

Open water from springs forms steam in the chill air but does not impede travel. Wander up the valley, enjoying the pastel colors of a midwinter day reflected in the waters of the creek's channels. Carry a thermos of hot chocolate and have a winter picnic.

Dress warmly and take extra clothing. Although the valley opens to the south, receiving what sunlight is available, downslope breezes off the mountainsides are chilly. Occasional williwaw winds can blow quite strongly. Portage Lake can also be quite windy, but don't let this discourage you from taking the trip. Since Bear Valley is at right angles to local prevailing winds, it may be still even when Portage is windblown. In the valley's quiet air, delicate frost often hangs on the trees. Do not travel near the ice cliffs of Portage Glacier; in winter the glacier calves from the bottom, sending waves which break up the lake ice near the glacier.

Portage Lake and Bear Valley are closed to off-road vehicles year-round.

PORTAGE TO POTTER

21 Portage Pass

Round trip to viewpoint 5 miles, to glacier
    and overlook 9 miles
Hiking time 3–7 hours
High point 750 feet
Total elevation gain to viewpoint 750 feet,
    to overlook 1100 feet in, 500 feet out
Best July–September
USGS map Seward D5
Chugach National Forest

Hop the train to Whittier, prepared for a steep, but easy uphill hike, good for all ages. Look forward to spectacular views of Passage Canal, Portage Glacier, and surrounding mountains and glaciers.

The strategic location of Portage Pass, on the isthmus between Turnagain Arm and ice-free Passage Canal, gave it an historic role. Hundreds of years ago Indians, Eskimos, and Russians used it as a trading route, crossing Portage Glacier from the pass; at that time Portage Lake had not yet formed.

Following the discovery of gold in the Turnagain Arm area in 1890, Alaska's first gold rush began, later to be followed by a stampede to the more distant gold of the Iditarod area. When Cook Inlet was clogged by ice floes, ships would drop prospectors at Passage Canal. The approach to the glacier was so steep that ropes and pulleys were required to pull heavily loaded sleds up the grade. Portage Pass is also a major route for migrating birds, including arctic terns, sandhill cranes, swans, ducks, and geese.

Getting to Whittier on Passage Canal is an excursion in itself. Not accessible by road, the town is served by the Alaska Railroad, which runs a shuttle from Anchorage and Portage daily in the summer and several times a week the rest of the year. Cars may be taken on the train but are not needed for this hike. To reach Whittier, drive to the Portage railroad ramp, mile 80, Seward Highway (47 miles south of Anchorage). Foot passengers park in the south area; those taking cars on the train should follow signs for ferry traffic at the north entrance. The train goes through two tunnels before reaching Whittier. The trail starts near the second tunnel exit, but the train continues 1½ miles farther. (Subtract 3 miles from the hike distance if you drive to the trailhead from Whittier.)

From the train, walk the gravel road, which heads west, paralleling the tracks, almost to the tank farm near the tunnel. Take the only road that goes left across the tracks (elevation about 50 feet). Park here if you are driving.

Follow the right-hand fork of the road past the shell of a white house and continue up a steep old road. At the pass trees are left behind and the old road goes through a little pond. Bear right up a small promontory (elevation 750 feet) for a view of Portage Glacier and Carpathian Peak. This is a fine picnic spot and, for many, a good destination.

To reach the glacier, a mile away, follow the old road down to Divide Lake and travel left around it. Well before the lake's outlet, head down the slope to the glacier. Alders are thick near the outlet stream but pose little problem over much of the slope southeast of it. Watch for black bears. Elevation loss is about 500 feet.

For a magnificent overview of Portage Glacier, its ice cliffs, and the lake, walk up the outlet stream until the cliffs on the opposite side can be climbed easily via a rocky chute to a bench of bedrock. Work through patchy alders to a ledge above the glacier terminus and sit awhile. You may see ice fall from the glacier into Portage Lake. Burns Glacier lies to the left, east of Portage Glacier.

Water and campsites are readily available. Watch the weather carefully as Por-

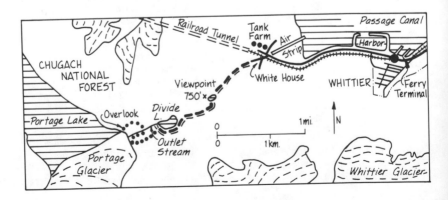

Portage Glacier and Lake, October (Simmerman photo)

tage Pass can be a wind funnel. Even so, wind at Whittier, particularly from the west, does not always mean wind at the pass. Whittier has the second highest recorded annual precipitation in Alaska, 175 inches. The greatest snow depth measured in Whittier was 141 inches; at the pass it can be 250 inches or more. Although the pass is low in elevation, snow often remains through June.

Avalanche hazard makes this trip dangerous in winter and spring. The trail is closed to off-road vehicles from April 1 through June 30.

PORTAGE TO POTTER

22 Alyeska Glacier View

Via chairlift: round trip hike ⅔ mile
Hiking time 1-2 hours
High point 2750 feet
Elevation gain 310 feet
Best July-September

Via foot: round trip 6 miles to the 3939-foot "summit"
Hiking time 4-8 hours
High point 3939 feet
Elevation gain 3600 feet
Best July-September
USGS map Seward D6
Chugach National Forest

For an easy romp with the children, summer skiing, or technical mountaineering—all with a beautiful view of Turnagain Arm and Glacier Valley—go to Mt. Alyeska. The chairlift can make this an easy outing. Check with Alyeska Resort for lift rates and schedule (address and phone number in the Appendix). Watch for marmots, parka squirrels, and mountain goats. Skiing is often possible on the glacier and upper parts of the mountain through June.

At mile 90, Seward Highway (37 miles south of Anchorage), turn north onto Alyeska Highway and drive 3 miles to Alyeska Resort's parking area. Take the chairlift, which operates daily during the summer tourist season, to the top (elevation 2540 feet). Climb the knob above the sun deck and restaurant (food and drink available) and continue up the ridge to a view of tiny Alyeska Glacier. Relax, play, picnic, soak up the magnificent view on the heather-covered mountainside. Join the children sliding down the steep slopes or glissading on snow patches. Be sure to find out when the chairlift closes.

Hikers who feel that chairlifts are an unethical way to reach timberline can certainly walk! From the ski lodge (elevation 340 feet), look for tracked-vehicle trails that climb the ski slopes. These lead to the sun deck and restaurant at the top of Chair 1. Climb either the Racing Trail on the north side of Alyeska Creek or the more gentle trail through the Bowl south of the creek. The hiker can cross from one trail to the other part way up, traversing between the base of Chair 2 (which starts in the Bowl) and mid-station on Chair 1. From the sun deck, continue up the ridge to a view of the glacier. A popular outing is to ride the chairlift up and walk back down.

The more adventurous may wish to climb to the apparent summit of Mt. Alyeska (elevation 3939 feet). Two routes are possible: (1) continue up the ridge you followed to view the glacier; (2) from the sun deck, hike down to cross Alyeska Creek and climb Center Ridge, which begins near the creek in the Bowl. Both routes have

Sun deck and Turnagain Arm from route to Alyeska Glacier, August (Simmerman photo)

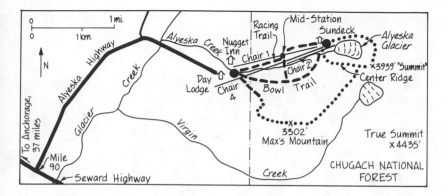

spots where the novice may prefer a rope belay. Descend by either route or follow the southwest ridge around the Bowl to point 3302, locally known as "Max's Mountain." No trail exists down Max's, but the descent is not difficult. From point 3302, bear due west to avoid cliffs, then descend to a bench covered with low vegetation. Follow this to the right until an opening appears in the alders and continue downward to the ski slope. Allow 3 to 6 hours from the top of the chairlift to the "summit" of Mt. Alyeska and down by this route, a distance of about 5 miles.

In season salmonberries and blueberries can be found along these trails. Snow is the only water high on the mountain; Alyeska Creek is silty. Climbing on the glacier and the ridge traverse to point 4435, the true summit, should be attempted only by experienced mountaineers.

Recreational use of off-road vehicles and mountain bicycles on the ski slopes and maintenance-vehicle trails is prohibited at all times.

PORTAGE TO POTTER

23 Winner Creek Trail

Gorge: round trip 7 miles
Hiking time 4–6 hours
High point 600 feet
Total elevation gain 260 feet in, 200 feet out
Best May–October
USGS map Seward D6

Upper Winner Creek Trail: round trip 18 miles
Allow 2 days
High point 2855 feet
Elevation gain 2515 feet
Best June–October
USGS map Seward D6
Chugach National Forest

A pleasant trail at the base of Mt. Alyeska through tall spruce and hemlock trees leads to the plunging waters of Winner Creek gorge. Walk with history here on a portion of the old Iditarod Trail, which went from Seward over Crow Pass. A branch of the trail leads toward the headwaters of Winner Creek, with access to the Twentymile country and other intriguing areas. Watch for moose and bears. The trail offers excellent ski touring.

Winner Creek gorge, August (Simmerman photo)

At mile 90, Seward Highway (37 miles south of Anchorage), turn north onto Alyeska Highway and drive 3 miles to Alyeska Resort's parking lot.

Walk to the north end of the Nugget Inn, past the upper condominiums and up onto the ski slope. The trail begins just beyond the base of the rope tow (elevation 350 feet). Ferns, blueberry bushes, and moss carpet the forest floor beneath the tall conifers. The trail crosses pleasant creeks and short sections of muskeg. (Wear waterproof boots.) A number of side trails intersect, part of a cross-country ski racing system; follow the pink ribbons marking the hiking trail for the most direct route.

About 2½ miles from Alyeska Resort, the hiking trail intersects two trails. Continue to the second intersection, which is on the side of Winner Creek's steep wooded canyon. Be sure you can identify this intersection on the return trip. The left

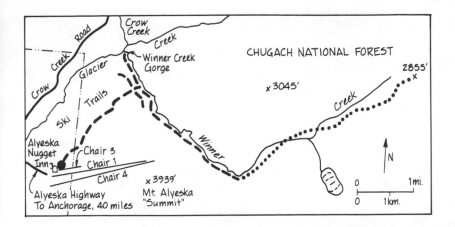

branch goes to Winner Creek gorge (elevation 400 feet), less than a mile away and well worth the walk. The right branch leads up Winner Creek, wandering through meadows, alder, willow patches, and cottonwood forests en route. It may be necessary to wade in the stream occasionally to avoid brush. Walking is good from brushline at about 1500 feet on to point 2855 at the head of the valley.

Except for the upper reaches of Winner Creek, the trails are gentle, with no severe ups or downs. Water is regularly available along both trails. Upper Winner Creek has many tempting tent sites.

The ski trails are not maintained, but after each snowfall tracks are usually set by usage. Numerous loops exist, utilizing parts of the first 2 miles of the summer hiking trail. The trail to Winner Creek gorge makes a good day ski trip. Upper Winner Creek is not recommended because of potential avalanches. (See "Avalanches," page 24.)

Most skiers, especially when snowfall is lean, prefer to ski the meadows below the hiking trail, starting at the end of Arlberg Avenue, two blocks north of the resort. Park at the resort to avoid inconveniencing residents along the narrow street. On any ski trail, be careful not to destroy the center ridge between the ski tracks and, please, no boots, snowshoes, dogs, or snowmobiles on the ski trail.

Winner Creek trail and the National Forest lands in Glacier Valley are closed to horses and off-road vehicles, including snowmobiles, year-round.

PORTAGE TO POTTER

24 Glacier Creek Ski Tour

Round trip up to 12 miles
Skiing time 3–10 hours
High point 800 feet
Total elevation gain 650 feet
Best December–February
USGS maps Seward D6, Anchorage A6
Chugach National Forest

To visit an intriguing canyon accessible only in winter, ski frozen Glacier Creek beneath towering snow-hung cliffs. Immobile waterfalls—cascades of ice—form trailside sculptures. Because the stream surface is smooth and climbs very gently,

83

Ski touring on Glacier Creek, January (Simmerman photo)

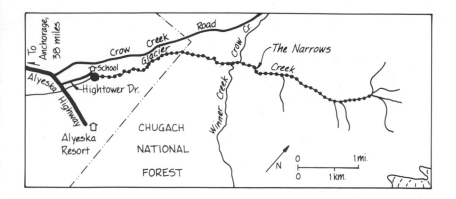

the trip is excellent for beginning skiers. Do not attempt to walk the route because there may be pockets of thin ice.

At mile 90, Seward Highway (37 miles south of Anchorage), turn north onto Alyeska Highway and drive 2.25 miles to Hightower Drive, just before Glacier Creek bridge. Turn left and continue north to the Girdwood school, leaving the car at the school parking area (elevation 150 feet).

On skis, head east to Glacier Creek and follow the stream upvalley to the northeast. Certain portions of the creek near the school and the Alyeska Highway bridge seldom freeze over even when the canyon section of the creek is skiable. So give the route a try before deciding it is not possible. About 3 miles from the school, Winner Creek enters from the right in a frozen waterfall; shortly after, Crow Creek comes in from the left.

The skier has a river-level view of the canyon. Note the lovely hoarfrost crystals growing in ice caverns above open water. If time allows, continue up Glacier Creek beyond the entry of Crow Creek, to the Narrows, the most scenic part of the canyon. Beyond the Narrows the valley opens, surrounded by the hanging glaciers and snowy peaks, Glacier Creek's headwaters.

Hoarfrost crystals on Glacier Creek ice, February (Simmerman photo)

Dress warmly; sun seldom reaches the canyon bottom in the winter and a cool breeze drains from the mountains almost any time of year. A thermos of hot bouillon hits the spot at rest time on the trail.

This trip is suggested only for the coldest months, when Glacier Creek is most likely to be well frozen; some years the weather is too warm for a good ice cover. On skis or snowshoes, weight is so well distributed that the danger of breaking through the ice is slight. Be cautious of thin ice, however, testing questionable spots first with a ski pole, then with a hard stamp of the ski. Generally the depth of the water beneath you is not great. If a ski trail is already established, snowshoers should make their own trail. Snowshoes break down the ridge between ski tracks, eliminating the advantage of a ski trail.

Glacier Creek is closed at all times to off-road vehicles.

PORTAGE TO POTTER

25 Crow Pass

Round trip 8 miles; traverse 25 miles
Hiking time 4–6 hours; traverse 2–3 days
High point 3600 feet
Total elevation gain 2000 feet northbound,
  3050 feet southbound
Best mid-June–September
USGS maps Anchorage A6, A7
Chugach National Forest, Chugach State Park

Crow Pass offers a pleasant day trip into a beautiful mountain wilderness with gold mine relics, glaciers, an alpine lake, and wildflowers. Walk a dogsled route once traveled by mail carriers, explorers and prospectors. Experienced hikers can take a 2- or 3-day trip on the old Iditarod Trail to Eagle River.

In the early 1900s, the trail over Crow Pass was part of the Iditarod winter sled trail through the mountains between Turnagain and Knik arms. The route led from Seward to Knik and thence to Interior gold fields. It was used alternately with the Indian Pass Trail (Trip 27), the preferred route. Steady use of both trails probably ended in the early 1920s, when regular railroad service began between Seward and Fairbanks.

The old mail trail over Crow Pass continued down Raven Creek and out Eagle

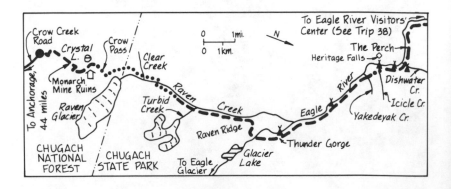

Crystal Lake at Crow Pass, July (Simmerman Photo)

River. Trail work has opened up an excellent 2-3 day trip, although uncertain trail conditions make allowing 3 days advisable. Contact the Chugach State Park office (address in the Appendix) for current trail information and to file a trip plan, if desired.

At mile 90, Seward Highway (37 miles south of Anchorage), turn north onto Alyeska Highway. As the highway rounds a curve to the right at mile 2, turn left onto Crow Creek Road. Continue 5.8 miles to the road's end at a parking area (elevation 1550 feet). The trailhead is marked.

On foot, follow the old mining road as it climbs in switchbacks to brushline. At 2500 feet elevation, 1.7 miles from the parking area, are the ruins of the Monarch Mine, a hard-rock gold mine that operated from 1906-1948. The trail passes remains of a mill and crew's quarters; above, in the cliffs, are mine adits. Walk uphill behind the mine ruins for a side trip along the flume bed into the beautiful canyon through which Crow Creek cascades.

To reach Crow Pass, follow the steep trail up the switchbacks above the mine ruins toward the pass. At mile 3 (elevation 3500 feet) a U.S. Forest Service A-frame cabin is available for public use. Make reservations through a Forest Service office (addresses in the Appendix). The cabin is not rented during winter and early spring because of avalanche hazard; moreover, it has no heating stove.

Nearby Crystal Lake, nestled beneath a steep mountain wall and rimmed by wildflowers, is a splendid destination for many. West of the lake lies the tip of Crow Glacier. To see Raven Glacier, about a mile farther, hike north past the cabin, following rock cairns through the pass (elevation 3600 feet). Look for Dall sheep and mountain goats.

Camping spots abound in both the mine and pass areas. Water is available; campfires are not permitted. Snow showers and strong winds are possible any time, so take a parka, cap, and mittens. The trail is extremely hazardous in winter because of avalanche danger. (See "Avalanches," page 24.)

To complete the traverse to Eagle River, follow the cairn-marked trail from the Raven Glacier overlook down the moraine bench on the southwestern side of the glacier. Continue toward a big gravel bar, staying on the west side of Raven Creek until reaching the bar. Cross Clear Creek (bridged) at its junction with Raven Creek. In ½ mile cross Raven Creek on a bridge located at the lower end of the gravel bar and just above a gorge. Note the natural stone arch at the bottom of the waterfall in the gorge. From this point to the Eagle River Visitors' Center, hikers frequently see bears. (See "Moose and bears," page 19.)

The trail now parallels the east side of Raven Creek for about 3 miles, staying on

Eagle Glacier and Glacier Lake, August (Simmerman photo)

the hillside above it. In a mile, cross Turbid Creek on a bridge. Clear drinking water is not likely to be available along this stretch. The trail sometimes lies on the historic trail bed and sometimes parallel to it. Where the trail crosses Raven Ridge, there is a view of Eagle Glacier and, using binoculars, the marked fording area to cross Eagle River.

The trail continues steeply down Raven Ridge toward Eagle River. When you reach level ground, turn right, heading toward Eagle Glacier. A good river-crossing area is well marked about ¼ mile upstream from the moraine piles and ½ mile downstream from Glacier Lake. (Elevation of crossing is 850 feet.) Although instructions on how to ford are posted, practice crossing streams before taking on this swift glacial river. (See "Stream crossings," page 18.) Expect knee-deep water. Despite the river's glacial origin, its water level does not rise greatly late in the day. Heavy rain storms, however, will cause the water level to rise rapidly. If the river is too high to cross safely, camp and wait.

From the ford, the trail parallels the river, passing Thunder Gorge in about 1½ miles. The next stretch of trail, traversing the cliff close to the river, is potentially hazardous because the trail is in danger of being eroded by high water. From the river crossing it is about 6 miles to Icicle Creek and about 11 miles to Eagle River Visitors' Center and the trail's end (elevation 500 feet).

Look for cairns when crossing the braids of Icicle Creek. The trail continues past a raspberry patch (watch for bears here in berry season) and across Dishwater Creek to connect with the trail described under Trip 38, The Perch. Many good campsites are to be found along the way, but campfires are permitted only in established firepits or on the gravel bars of Eagle River. Firearms may be carried for self-protection; target shooting is prohibited.

A copy of a topographic map showing the trail is available for viewing at the Chugach State Park office or at the Eagle River Visitors' Center. The entire trail is closed to off-road vehicles, including snowmobiles. The state park section of the trail is closed to horses, pack animals, and bicycles year-round; the portion in the Chugach National Forest is closed to horses from April 1 to June 30. The Visitors' Center has a public pay phone.

PORTAGE TO POTTER

26 Bird Ridge

Round trip 2–12 miles
Hiking time 1–8 hours
High point 4650 feet
Total elevation gain 4600 feet
Best April–October
USGS maps Seward D7, Anchorage A7
Chugach State Park

Take a picnic lunch in the spring, climb as high as desired, stretch out on the ground, and enjoy the warm sunshine and rich smell of earth—all while surrounding mountains remain cloaked in white. Because of its southern exposure, Bird Ridge sports the earliest spring flowers and has become the standard spring conditioner for locals. The hike is steep but worth the effort because of its sweeping view of fjordlike Turnagain Arm.

To reach the trailhead (elevation 50 feet), drive to mile 102.1, Seward Highway (25 miles south of Anchorage), and turn north into a large off-road parking area (marked). The trail climbs through a pleasant birch forest to meet a powerline/pipeline ac-

Turnagain Arm from Bird Ridge, May (Simmerman photo)

cess road. Turn right and follow the road about ¼ mile to the ridge crest, just beyond the pipeline arrow sign. Ahead spread the valleys of Bird and Penguin creeks. The Bird Ridge foot trail continues left up the crest of the ridge.

Soon brush is left behind. The first high point (elevation 3505 feet) is a good destination for a short trip. In early spring it may be necessary to skirt snow patches. The energetic can continue 4 miles farther to point 4650, overlooking the headwaters of Ship Creek. The ridge culminates at 4960 feet.

Whether you gain point 3505, point 4650, or just stop at the powerline (elevation 400 feet), the views of the surrounding mountains and Turnagain Arm are magnificent. Turnagain Arm was named by Captain James Cook in 1778, when he explored these waters as part of his search for the Northwest Passage.

Turnagain Arm has one of the world's greatest tide differentials, with a range of as

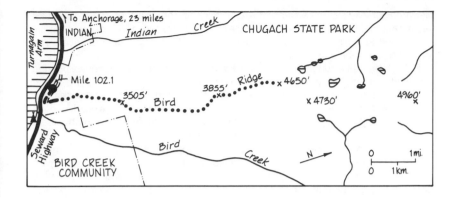

much as 37 feet. Watch for tidal bores, the well-defined leading wave of an incoming tide. The Arm was scoured out by glaciers and has since been filled by silt carried by streams from the retreating rivers of ice. At low tide these mud flats are clearly visible. Because of the speed of the tide as it pours into and out of the narrow Arm and because of frequent high winds, the waters are dangerous for small boats.

Look for the season's first Jacob's ladders and anemones, followed by the flowering of the whole cycle of dry tundra plants. Ptarmigan and Dall sheep are frequent visitors to the ridge.

The footing is excellent, and though the hike steep in spots, it is not unpleasantly so. No drinking water is available along the trail. The best camping is at the Bird Creek Campground; campfires are permitted only in the campground. Winter hiking on the ridge can be excellent, but stay on the ridge crest to avoid avalanches. (See "Avalanches," page 24.)

The trail is closed to off-road vehicles year-round.

PORTAGE TO POTTER

27 Indian Valley

Round trip 12 miles; traverse 21 miles
Hiking time 7 hours; traverse 3 days
High point 2350 feet
Total elevation gain 2100 feet northbound;
   1250 feet traverse southbound
Best May–October; winter: February–March
USGS maps Seward D7, Anchorage A7
Chugach State Park

Indian Valley offers a good family hike along Indian Creek through a delightful combination of forests and meadows to alpine tundra and tiny lakes high in the mountains. In the early 1900s mushers drove their dogs from Indian to Ship Creek. They crossed over Indian Creek Pass, a part of the Iditarod Trail from Seward to Interior gold fields. The route was used alternately with Crow Pass (Trip 25). The Indian Creek section of the trail has been cleared and marked; the Ship Creek section is brushy, often boggy and sometimes difficult to find.

The trip up Indian Valley is also a pleasant ski tour; hardy skiers may want to make the entire traverse, starting from Arctic Valley Road.

To reach the trailhead from the community of Indian, turn north at mile 103.1,

91

Seward Highway (25 miles south of Anchorage), on the gravel road just west of a restaurant and Indian Creek. After 0.5 mile take the right fork and continue 0.8 mile, turning left at the pump station, to the road's end. Park in the area provided. The trailhead (elevation 250 feet) is marked.

Follow the trail through tall conifer trees and cross delightful meadows created by winter avalanches. (Beware of these open places in winter and spring during periods of high avalanche danger. See "Avalanches," page 24.) The trail can be wet, so waterproof or well-greased boots are recommended. Plan to ford a creek about 4 miles from the trailhead. At the ford trees are left behind; ahead, high tundra beckons. The entire trail climbs gently, with no steep ups or downs.

The pass is an old moraine, its knobs and dips well-vegetated by scrub hemlock and crowberries. Nearby ridges and side valleys with tiny alpine lakes invite exploration. Larger Ship Lake is 3½ miles away, over Indian Pass and southwest up Ship Creek, along a route that connects with the Ramp (Trip 32). Camping in the pass is ideal. Water is plentiful; campfires are not permitted, so bring a stove.

Indian Creek Pass, September (Simmerman photo)

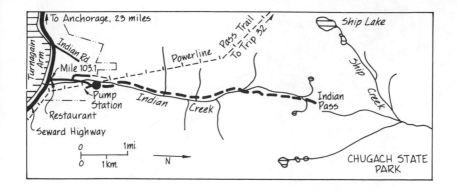

If you are planning to hike to the Ship Creek trailhead (15 miles farther), check first with the Chugach State Park office for trail conditions and directions. While the alpine section has been well marked with yellow poles, the lower end of the trail, going through bogs and vast areas of brush, is unmarked. Traces of the old Iditarod Trail can still be found, however. Ruins of a roadhouse are on the west side of Ship Creek, about a mile above its confluence with the North Fork.

A ford across Ship Creek about ½ mile north of the North Fork confluence is clearly marked. Southbound hikers and skiers should find this site and follow the marked route to the pass to avoid entering the North Fork by mistake. A number of hikers and skiers have unwittingly taken this seriously wrong turn.

The Ship Creek trailhead (elevation 1950 feet) is at mile 6.5, Arctic Valley Road. (See map, Trip 36.) Look for a "Turnout" sign at the parking area. A trail drops nearly to the level of the creek, then parallels it to Indian Pass. In winter, the 21-mile trip can take 3 days if extensive trail-breaking is necessary; if spring snow conditions are ideal, strong skiers can make the trip in 1 day. With a heavy pack, the novice skier may have difficulty negotiating the tight turns descending through wooded Indian Valley.

The Powerline Pass Trail, described in Trip 32, terminates in Indian Valley, but the trailhead is different from that of the Indian Creek Trail. (See map.) Do not attempt the Powerline Pass Trail in winter due to extreme avalanche hazard.

Indian Creek Trail is closed to off-road vehicles year-round.

PORTAGE TO POTTER

28 Table Rock

Round trip 2 miles or more
Hiking time 1-2 hours
High point 1083 feet
Total elevation gain 980 feet
Best April-October
USGS map Anchorage A8

Snow is soon gone from this south-facing slope, making it one of the nicest spring hikes in the area. The lower part of the trail can often be hiked as early as April; wildflowers abound and are in bloom by mid-May. Brilliant autumn colors grace the mountainside in late September. Watch for red squirrels, varying hares,

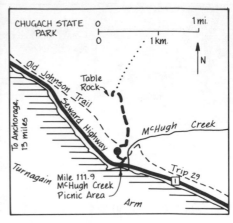

Dall sheep ewe (Simmerman photo)

parka squirrels, moose, and migrating birds. The lower part of the trail passes through a pleasant woods of spruce, aspen and cottonwood. Views of Turnagain Arm are spectacular.

The steep trail to Table Rock is good for children used to hiking uphill. Footgear with good traction is recommended since the well-worn path is slippery when wet. Beyond Table Rock the hike becomes very steep and in one place is a rock scramble. No water is available.

From the intersection of Northern Lights Boulevard and the Seward Highway in Anchorage, drive south on the Seward Highway about 14 miles to mile 111.9, McHugh Creek Picnic Area. Follow the entrance road and take the left fork to the upper parking lot (elevation 100 feet). (Note that the gate to the picnic area is locked each night at 9 p.m. Alternate parking is provided below the gate beside the Seward Highway.)

On foot, follow the Old Johnson Trail (marked) a short distance to a fork in the trail. Take the right-hand trail, following it along the base of the mountain to the bank above McHugh Creek. From here the trail climbs more or less directly uphill; ignore side trails leading down to McHugh Creek. Ascend a rocky outcropping and continue upward, leaving McHugh Creek behind.

Jacob's ladder, lupine, violets, high bush cranberry, bearberry, columbine, wild geranium, dwarf dogwood, wild rose, pyrola and other wildflowers grace the trail side. On windless days delightful rocky promontories lure the hiker to rest. The hike is pleasant on windy days as well, since the route is well protected by trees.

After climbing through forest for about ½ hour, watch for an obvious rocky promontory, Table Rock. From it, the view of Turnagain Arm and the Kenai Mountains beyond is superb, destination enough for a picnic or an evening.

To continue to the ridge above, find a trail from Table Rock through the woods. The trail leads to an extremely steep, narrow dirt track up the cliffs. The climbing is not technical, but it may be necessary to use the rocks and trees for handholds. Test the holds before using them! As you leave the timber, note your surroundings and line them up with landmarks below to help in finding the way back down. Continue upward, picking your own route and destination. Allow 5–7 hours round trip to the ridge.

The trail is closed to off-road vehicles year-round.

Turnagain Arm from Table Rock, September (Nienhueser photo)

PORTAGE TO POTTER

29 Old Johnson Trail

One way 11 miles
Hiking time 5-8 hours
High point 900 feet
Total elevation gain 1130 feet eastbound,
   1375 feet westbound
Best April-November
USGS maps Anchorage A8(SE),
   Seward D7, D8
Chugach State Park

For an eagle's-eye view of Turnagain Arm, stroll the Old Johnson Trail and find the first wildflowers of spring. Watch for beluga (white) whales and Dall sheep. The trail, originally developed in 1910 as a telegraph line, predates Anchorage and was used as an alternate mail trail from Seward to Knik, when snow conditions necessitated. The main winter trails went over Crow Pass (Trip 25) and Indian Pass (Trip 27).

The Old Johnson Trail offers opportunities for good family outings and can be hiked in short or long segments. South of McHugh Creek, during periods of new and full moons, watch for tidal bores 1½–2 hours after the Anchorage low tide. (Check newspapers for tide times.) Snow is seldom deep enough for skiing, so the trail often provides good winter hiking. Historically the trail extended beyond Girdwood, but southeast of Windy Corner the trail is obscured by natural land sluffing and highway construction.

McHugh Creek Picnic Area, May—Trips 28 and 29 (Simmerman photo)

Horses and sledge on the Old Johnson Trail, from an early photo (Photo courtesy The Alaska Railroad)

To reach the western trailhead at Potter, drive to mile 115.1, Seward Highway, 10.7 miles south of the intersection of Northern Lights Boulevard and the Seward Highway in Anchorage. Just south of the Potter railroad section house, turn up a steep dirt road and drive 0.4 mile to the first switchback. Park off the roadway. In winter, since portions of the access road are often covered with overflow ice, park at the beginning of the road near the highway.

The Potter trailhead (1)—elevation 312 feet—is marked. Portions of the trail are wet in spring. The McHugh Creek Picnic Area (2)—elevation gain 180 feet—is 3.5 miles southeast.

At McHugh Creek Picnic Area (elevation 100 feet), follow the paved road to the parking lot beside the creek. Walk the trail up the left side of the creek and cross the bridge. Just beyond the first switchback, an inconspicuous, but marked, trail goes right to Rainbow (3), 3.5 miles away (elevation gain 800 feet). From McHugh Creek, the trail climbs high above Turnagain Arm, emerging from the cottonwood forest to a panoramic view. Here the trail passes under high, rocky, rotten cliffs. Be sure no one is on the cliffs above, watch for natural rockfalls, and take care not to dislodge rocks because people may be below. Cliff scrambling here is dangerous.

Beyond the cliffs the trail enters pleasant woods. About 1½ miles from McHugh Creek, where a major creek drainage is on the right, the trail forks; take the upper fork. From here the trail again climbs, to about 900 feet, then descends in switchbacks, crossing gravel Rainbow Valley road and continuing downhill along Rainbow Creek to the Rainbow trailhead at mile 108.3, Seward Highway.

From the Rainbow trailhead parking area (elevation 10 feet), the trail climbs a gentle grade and continues about 2 miles (4) (elevation gain 200 feet) to Windy Corner. A short trail leads down to mile 106.7, Seward Highway (elevation 10 feet).

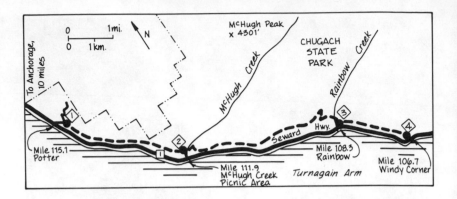

Westbound and shorter trip directions:

McHugh Creek Picnic Area access (2), mile 111.9, Seward Highway. To hike to the Potter trailhead (3½ miles, elevation gain 325 feet) take the left fork on the picnic area road to the upper parking area. The trail, which leaves from the upper end of the parking area, is marked.

Rainbow Valley access (3), mile 108.3, Seward Highway. Park in the area provided north of the highway. Walk west to the trailhead (marked) on the east bank of Rainbow Creek. McHugh Creek Picnic Area is 4 miles away (gain 850 feet).

Windy Corner (4), mile 106.7, Seward Highway. Park at the pullout on the north side of the highway and climb the boulder-covered slope, bearing left to connect with the obvious old trail at the base of the rock cliffs. Follow the Old Johnson Trail west to Rainbow Valley (2 miles, gain 200 feet).

The trail is closed to off-road vehicles year-round.

Top: left, *bunchberry or ground dogwood in July;* right, *blueberries, September.*
Below: left, Amanita muscaria, *a poisonous mushroom, September;* right, *fern, September. (Simmerman photos)*

Friendly parka (arctic ground) squirrel (Simmerman photo)

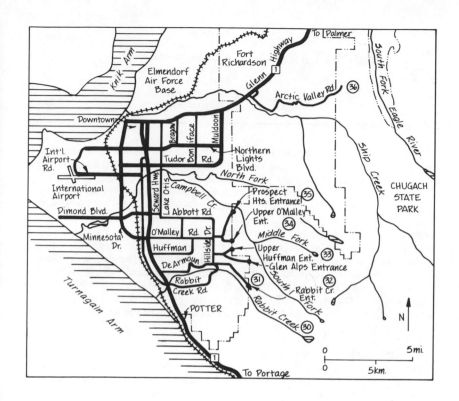

ANCHORAGE BOWL

30 Rabbit Lake 102
31 Flattop 103
32 The Ramp 105
33 Williwaw Lakes. 107
34 Wolverine Peak 109
35 Knoya and Tikishla Peaks 111
36 Rendezvous Peak 113

30 Rabbit Lake

Round trip 11 miles
Hiking time 5–8 hours
High point 3082 feet
Total elevation gain 1280 feet
Best June–October
USGS maps Anchorage A7, A8(SE)
Chugach State Park

With blue-black waters below 2000-foot walls of the dramatic Suicide Peaks, Rabbit Lake is the most accessible alpine lake in the Anchorage vicinity and a scenic delight. The valley is an excellent place to take the children camping.

From the intersection of Northern Lights Boulevard and the Seward Highway, drive south on the Seward Highway 7 miles to DeArmoun Road. Turn left (east) toward the mountains and drive 3.5 miles to its intersection with Hillside Drive. Continue straight across Hillside Drive onto Upper DeArmoun Road. Follow it 1 mile, bear right onto Lower Canyon Road and continue, often climbing steeply, another 1.2 miles to Echo Drive and the Chugach State Park boundary. The road, maintained about another ½ mile, continues into the Park as Upper Canyon Road. Vehicles should park along Upper Canyon Road without blocking traffic (very limited parking, elevation 1490 feet). Though the road is open for another 3 miles to motorized vehicles (permitted on the road only), it deteriorates drastically and should be attempted only by four-wheel-drive vehicles with high clearance. Rabbit Lake lies about 5½ miles from the park boundary and 2 miles from the end of the road.

From the four-wheel-drive parking area at the end of the road (elevation 2900 feet) hike parallel to a muddy jeep track across the tundra to the lake. This track is an ugly and unnecessary scar marring an otherwise lovely valley. Now that the area is part of the Chugach State Park, use of vehicles beyond the end of the established road is prohibited. Report license numbers of offending vehicles and descriptions of the drivers to the Park office (address in the Appendix).

The lake lies at the base of the Suicide Peaks (elevations 5005 and 5065 feet), which are linked by the high saddle of Windy Gap. On windless days, camping here is delightful. Swimmers have been known to try the lake. Nevertheless, carry warm clothing; winds can be fierce. No campfires are permitted, so bring a stove.

While the Suicides are not technical climbs, neither are they easy hikes. Several easier side trips beckon the hiker. One is to climb up the ridge to the northeast. Just beyond the four-wheel-drive parking area this ridge drops to a broad pass at 3585 feet. Climb 600 feet to this pass and visit the small tarn nestled below the 1300-foot northwest flank of Ptarmigan Peak.

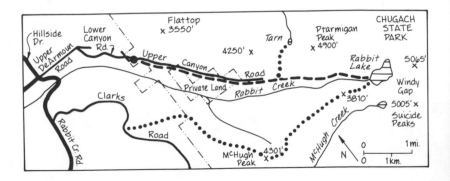

Rabbit Lake, July (Simmerman photo)

A second inviting side trip is to climb the ridge dividing Rabbit Creek and McHugh Creek valleys. From Rabbit Lake, at 3082 feet, climb to the first high point (elevation 3810 feet), an easy ascent, then walk the ridge. McHugh Peak (elevation 4301 feet) is about 3 miles along this ridge from Rabbit Lake. To avoid retracing your steps, you can descend the ridge leading northwest from McHugh Peak, to reach Clarks Road, a distance of 3 miles. Follow the road northwest to mile 3, Rabbit Creek Road. Carry drinking water. Do not attempt to follow McHugh Creek to the Seward Highway at McHugh Creek Wayside because there is difficult bushwhacking in the last 2 miles.

Off-road vehicles are prohibited at all times except on the established road.

ANCHORAGE BOWL

31 Flattop

Round trip 4 miles
Hiking time 3–5 hours
High point 3510 feet
Total elevation gain 1280 feet
Best June–October
USGS map Anchorage A8(SE)
Chugach State Park, Anchorage Watershed

Thanks to easy access, Flattop is probably the most frequently climbed peak in Alaska, and the trip to the top has long been the classic afternoon hike near Anchorage. The view from the top extends from Denali (Mt. McKinley) in the northwest to Mt. Redoubt volcano in the southwest. Though parts of the climb are steep—over

Turnagain Arm and Kenai Peninsula from Flattop, August (Nienhueser photo)

loose rock and without a definite trail—the ascent is not difficult. Small children and novices may have problems, however. Boots with good traction are desirable.

On the shortest and longest nights of the year, the Mountaineering Club of Alaska holds overnight outings on the summit despite the lack of water. Flattop is a good winter climb for those properly equipped, but avalanches have killed people on the north and southwest slopes. Do not slide down snow-filled gullies. (See "Avalanches," page 24, and check with the Chugach State Park office about current snow conditions before making a winter climb.)

From its intersection with Northern Lights Boulevard, drive south on the Seward Highway 5 miles to O'Malley Road. Turn left (east) toward the mountains and drive about 4 miles to the intersection with Hillside Drive. Turn right onto Hillside Drive and continue 1 mile to Upper Huffman Road. Turn left, go 0.7 mile, and turn right onto Toilsome Hill Drive (in winter, tire chains are recommended). This road switch-

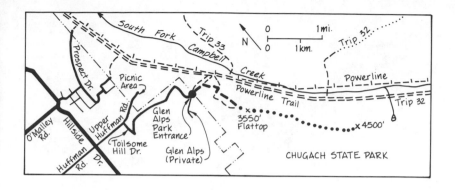

backs steeply uphill for about 2 miles to the Glen Alps entrance to Chugach State Park. Park here (elevation 2240 feet).

Many routes up Flattop are possible, but the following is recommended. From the parking lot, walk the upper of two trails, a dirt road, about 400 yards to a signpost and trail on the right. Take this right-hand trail, which leads toward Flattop. At an intersection with a major trail, turn right on it and traverse the slope, more or less paralleling the ridge. This leads to a gully from the low 2500-foot saddle which separates Flattop from the long low mound at the beginning of the ridge. The snow in this gully avalanches in winter. A well-defined trail leads up the northwest rock ridge to the left of the gully. In spring and early summer parts of the route are covered by snow.

From Flattop (elevation 3510 feet), the ridge can be followed 3 miles to its high point at 4500 feet. The route is exposed in some places, but an experienced hiker will encounter no real difficulty. For a circular route, return to the parking area by descending the steep northeast slope to the Powerline Trail.

Loose rock on the upper reaches of Flattop constitutes a serious potential hazard, and people have been injured here by falling rocks. Never roll rocks down the mountainside or allow children to do so. There may be people below, and even a small rock can become a lethal weapon. Avoid dislodging rocks and if one accidentally falls, immediately yell "Rock!" at the top of your voice and continue yelling until the rock is at rest.

The trail is closed to motorized vehicles year-round.

ANCHORAGE BOWL

32 The Ramp

Round trip 14 miles
Hiking time 8–10 hours
High point 5240 feet
Total elevation gain 3000 feet
Best June–September
USGS maps Anchorage A7, A8(SE)
Chugach State Park, Anchorage Watershed

On a sunny summer's day, take a delightfully easy hike to "Ship Lake Pass," then climb a 5240-foot peak. From the pass the mountainside does indeed resemble a ramp. The walk up is a moderately steep climb, gaining 1200 feet elevation in about

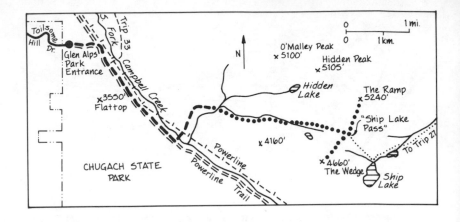

½ mile. From the top there are fine views, especially of the Ship Creek headwaters. An easier summit is the Wedge (elevation 4660 feet) southwest of the pass. The trip to the pass is good for children or a ski tour.

From its intersection with Northern Lights Boulevard, drive south on the Seward Highway 5 miles to O'Malley Road. Turn left (east) toward the mountains and drive about 4 miles to the intersection with Hillside Drive. Turn right onto Hillside Drive and continue 1 mile to Upper Huffman Road. Turn left, go 0.7 mile, and turn right onto Toilsome Hill Drive. (In winter tire chains are recommended for driving up Toilsome Hill Drive.) This road switchbacks steeply uphill for about 2 miles to the Glen Alps entrance to Chugach State Park. Park here (elevation 2240 feet).

On foot follow the lower of 2 trails ½ mile to a powerline. Turn right onto the powerline trail and follow it about 2 miles, past 13 power poles, to a point where an old jeep trail comes in from the left at right angles. Follow the jeep trail downhill to the South Fork of Campbell Creek. Normally the stream crossing is a rock-hop, but wading may be necessary at high water. The trail climbs the hill beyond the South Fork and continues through brush to cross the stream draining the valley ahead. Wander up the valley on the south side of the stream for easy, brush-free walking. After strolling to the pass (elevation 4050 feet, gain 1800 feet), enjoy the view, then follow the ridge north to the summit of the Ramp or south to the Wedge.

Walking in this alpine valley is freedom itself. The brush has been left behind and firm, dry tundra, laced with occasional springs, makes distances seem short. Look for wildflowers in season, parka squirrels, and Dall sheep. Enjoy the smell of heather on a warm sunny day. Visit Hidden Lake. Camping is inviting, but carry a cooking stove; campfires are prohibited in the park.

A 21-mile traverse to the community of Indian is possible (total elevation gain 1900 feet). From the east side of the pass, descend steeply to Ship Lake (elevation 2700 feet). Follow its outlet 1½ miles downstream, veer right around the corner, and follow the center fork of Ship Creek upstream to Indian Creek Pass (elevation 2350 feet). The trail from the pass to Indian is described in Trip 27.

Another traverse to Indian Valley is 13 miles long over Powerline Pass (elevation 3550 feet, gain 1300 feet), an easy walk up Powerline Trail. From the pass, the trail switches back down the steep slope into Indian Valley. The pass remains snowy into July, but when snow-free, it offers good camping near the streams to the southeast. The terminus for this trip differs from the beginning of the Indian Creek Pass trail. (See the map with Trip 27.) The Campbell Creek drainage and the trail north of a metal gate 2½ miles from Indian, is closed to off-road vehicles during snow-free months.

The Ramp, July (Simmerman photo)

Skiing and snowshoeing in the Campbell Creek drainage are inviting, but the area is open to snowmobiles when snow cover is sufficient. Under the right conditions, any of the slopes could avalanche, and snow-filled gullies pose a serious hazard, even when surrounding slopes are bare. (See "Avalanches," page 24.) The route over Powerline Pass should not be taken in winter due to extremely high avalanche hazard.

ANCHORAGE BOWL

33 Williwaw Lakes

Round trip 16 miles
Hiking time 10–12 hours
High point 3250 feet
Total elevation gain 1400 feet
Best June–early October
USGS maps Anchorage A7, A8(SE)
Chugach State Park, Anchorage Watershed

Alpine gems all different in size, color, shape, and setting, the lakes at the base of 5445-foot Mt. Williwaw lie in a mountain paradise. Walk amid a wide variety of alpine flowers on grassy meadows studded with scrub hemlock; pick blueberries,

*Toadstool (*Amanita muscaria*), August (Simmerman photo)*

cranberries, and crowberries in season. Families with older children who are ex-
perienced hikers will enjoy this as an overnight trip. The route includes part of the
Middle Fork Loop Trail, a popular hiking and ski-trail system connecting the Glen
Alps and Prospect Heights park entrances.

From the intersection of Northern Lights Boulevard and the Seward Highway,
drive south on the Seward Highway 5 miles to O'Malley Road. Turn left (east) toward
the mountains and drive about 4 miles to the intersection with Hillside Drive. Turn
right onto Hillside Drive and continue 1 mile to Upper Huffman Road. Turn left, go
0.7 mile, and turn right onto Toilsome Hill Drive (in winter, tire chains are recommended). This road switchbacks steeply uphill for about 2 miles to the Glen Alps entrance to Chugach State Park. Park here (elevation 2240 feet).

On foot, follow the lower of 2 trails ½ mile to a powerline. Turn right for about 300
yards on Powerline Trail, then left on a trail (marked with a sign for Middle Fork Loop
Trail) that leads downhill to the South Fork of Campbell Creek. Cross the stream on
rocks; if the water is high, wading may be necessary.

Once across the stream, follow a trail north (left) more or less paralleling the
stream. In about 1½ miles the trail forks. Follow the right-hand trail, heading up the
valley of the Middle Fork of Campbell Creek. When the trail ends, continue up the
valley, visiting lakes as you go. A nice destination is the final lake (elevation 3250
feet) in a cirque below Mt. Williwaw. If the weather is good plan to linger here, enjoying the solitude and magnificent scenery.

A 2-day, 19-mile circular trip continues from the cirque lake, over the low ridge

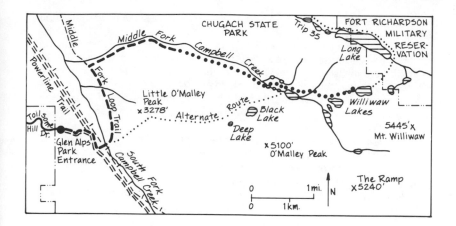

(elevation 3700 feet) above it to the northeast, and down to Long Lake and the valley of the North Fork of Campbell Creek. This valley can be followed past Tikishla and Knoya peaks to the Prospect Heights park entrance (Trip 35). Map-reading skills are essential to find the way out.

The hike to Williwaw Lakes is an excellent overnight trip for leisurely hikers. Campfires are prohibited in the Park, so bring a stove. The route also makes a good ski trip with access via the Middle Fork Loop Ski Trail from either the Glen Alps or the Prospect Heights entrance. Be aware of avalanche danger. (See "Avalanches," page 24.)

The entire area is closed to off-road vehicles year-round.

ANCHORAGE BOWL

34 Wolverine Peak

Round trip 11 miles
Hiking time 6–9 hours
High point 4455 feet
Total elevation gain 3340 feet
Best June–September; winter:
   November–April
USGS maps Anchorage A7, A8(NE)
Chugach State Park, Anchorage Watershed

Wolverine, the broad triangular mountain on the skyline east of Anchorage, makes an excellent 1-day trip, offering views of Anchorage, Cook Inlet, the Alaska Range, and glimpses of the lake-dotted wild country behind the peak. An old homesteader's road, now part of the Chugach State Park trail system, makes a fine access to timberline for hiking and ski touring. Watch for parka squirrels, spruce grouse, moose, and, on rare occasions, a wolverine. Pick blueberries and cranberries in season.

From its intersection with Northern Lights Boulevard, drive south on the Seward Highway 5 miles to O'Malley Road. Turn left (east) toward the mountains and drive about 4 miles to the intersection with Hillside Drive. Turn left, then immediately right onto Upper O'Malley Road. Follow it 0.5 mile to a "T" intersection. Turn left onto Prospect Drive (sometimes called Prospect Place) and continue 1.1 miles to the Prospect Heights entrance to Chugach State Park and a parking area (elevation 1115 feet).

On foot, follow the trail (an old road) that heads east from the end of the parking area. In ¼ mile the trail meets a powerline; turn left and continue on the main trail to the South Fork of Campbell Creek. Cross a bridge and continue around a sharp switchback and up a hill. A side trail (an old road) that turns sharply right is part of the Middle Fork Loop Trail system. Continue past this trail to the next trail (again an old road) entering from the right, a little over a mile beyond the creek and 2⅓ miles from the parking area.

Follow this trail as it angles off uphill, starting at an elevation of 1330 feet. The distance from here to the peak is about 3 miles. The old road becomes a narrow foot path through blueberry bushes, then emerges above brushline, paralleling the north side of the ridge crest. Climb to the crest and continue to the peak. The summit (elevation 4455 feet) is not obvious much of the way. The hike to brushline is a pleasant evening outing with a fine view of Denali (Mt. McKinley).

Wolverine Peak from Anchorage, October (Simmerman photo)

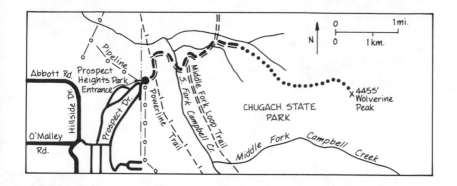

Climbers may want to tackle the peak in winter, though some avalanche hazard may exist. (See "Avalanches," page 24.) The upper slopes are likely to be wind-packed or windswept, and crampons may be necessary. The last part of the climb generally does not have enough snow for skiing.

A network of about 20 miles of ski trails is accessible from Prospect Heights and 3 other entrances to Chugach State Park. Ski the old road to its end beyond the Wolverine turnoff, or take the Middle Fork Loop Trail. The Loop Trail connects this entrance with Upper O'Malley, Upper Huffman, and Glen Alps park entrances and can be skied as a circular trip using the Powerline Trail. A leaflet showing the trail system is available from the Park office (address in the Appendix). Maps are also posted at trailheads.

The area is closed to off-road vehicles year-round.

ANCHORAGE BOWL

35 Knoya and Tikishla Peaks

Knoya: round trip 14 miles
Hiking time 10–12 hours
High point 4600 feet
Total elevation gain 3525 feet
Best late June–September
USGS maps Anchorage A7, A8(NE)

Tikishla: round trip 18 miles
Allow 2 days
High point 5150 feet
Total elevation gain 4075 feet
Best late June–September
USGS maps Anchorage A7, A8(NE)
Chugach State Park, Anchorage
    Watershed, Fort Richardson Military
    Reservation

Three trips, none easy, begin with the same access. Two are climbs. Lower, closer, and easier, Knoya is reached via a long, steep climb to the crest of its north-west ridge. The route up Tikishla, more interesting, follows a 2-mile-long ridge far-ther upvalley or, alternatively, traverses from Knoya. Hikers will prefer, instead of

Tikishla and North Fork Campbell Creek, September (Nienhueser photo)

climbing, to follow the North Fork of Campbell Creek to 60-acre Long Lake, in a cirque high above timberline. The access to all 3 trips involves some bushwhacking.

From its intersection with Northern Lights Boulevard, drive south on the Seward Highway 5 miles to O'Malley Road. Turn left (east) toward the mountains and drive about 4 miles to the intersection with Hillside Drive. Turn left, then immediately right onto Upper O'Malley Road. Follow it 0.5 mile to a "T" intersection. Turn left onto Prospect Drive (sometimes called Prospect Place) and continue 1.1 miles to the Prospect Heights entrance to Chugach State Park and a parking area (elevation 1115 feet).

On foot, follow the trail (an old homesteader's road) which heads east from the end of the parking area. In ¼ mile the trail meets a powerline; turn left and continue on the main trail to the South Fork of Campbell Creek. Cross a bridge and continue to the end of the old road, 2.7 miles from the parking area, ignoring trails branching to the right.

At the end of the old road, continue northward, contouring around Near Point. Do

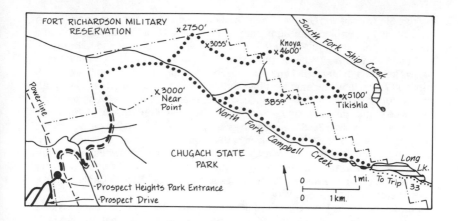

not follow a trail heading to the right (southeast) that climbs Near Point. Some bush-whacking may be necessary to gain the valley of the North Fork of Campbell Creek.

To reach Knoya, cross the North Fork and climb the ridge ahead, ascending to the notch just southeast of point 2750, the lowest of the three notches. Follow this ridge 2 miles to the summit of Knoya, the elevation gain is about 3000 feet from the stream crossing.

Tikishla's access lies 1 mile southeast (upvalley) of Knoya's, offering an inviting ridge to its summit with an elevation gain of 2950 feet from the base of the ridge. Both peaks lie within the Fort Richardson Military Reservation. A trip to Tikishla is best done as an overnight, camping near the stream at its base. Carry a stove since campfires are not permitted in the Park.

For an excellent circular route continue southeast past Long Lake, over the 3700-foot pass to Williwaw Lakes (Trip 33), and down the valley of the Middle Fork of Campbell Creek to the Prospect Heights trailhead.

The route up the North Fork is unsafe in winter due to avalanche hazard. (See "Avalanches," page 24.) The area is closed to off-road vehicles year-round.

ANCHORAGE BOWL

36 Rendezvous Peak

Round trip 3½ miles
Hiking time 2-5 hours
High point 4050 feet
Total elevation gain 1500 feet
Best anytime
USGS maps Anchorage A7, B7(SW)
Chugach State Park, Anchorage
    Watershed, Fort Richardson Military
    Reservation

To introduce children to mountains, Rendezvous Peak is a perfect first summit. Adults will enjoy the pleasant, easy climb, with spectacular views of Denali (Mt. McKinley), Mts. Foraker and Susitna, Cook Inlet, Turnagain and Knik arms, Anchorage, and the valleys of Ship Creek and Eagle River. In winter the trip to the pass is fun on cross-country skis, even for novices.

From 6th Avenue and Gambell Street in Anchorage, drive northeast on the Glenn Highway 6.3 miles and turn right onto Arctic Valley Road. (Southbound traffic should take the exit for Ft. Richardson at mile 8.1, Glenn Highway, and follow signs to Arctic Valley.) Drive 7 miles to the end of the road at the civilian ski area. Arctic Valley Road is a military road and may be closed at the base of the hill between 9 p.m. and 7 a.m. In winter studded tires or chains may be required for the steep ascent to Arctic Valley. From the parking lot (elevation 2550 feet) walk on the right-hand side of the stream up the valley to the northeast. A footpath leads to the pass.

The pass (elevation 3468 feet) has fine views, but those from the top of Rendezvous Peak (elevation 4050 feet) are even better. A steep but short ascent up the ridge to the right (south) of the pass leads to the craggy summit. Sit awhile to enjoy the view. From the top, the ridge extending southeast beckons, promising a walk in the clouds high above the valleys of Ship Creek and the South Fork of Eagle River. Be sure to carry water if you go very far.

From Rendezvous Peak choose your own descent route. For the young at heart, the tundra-covered slopes invite rolling or sliding down the soft natural carpet. In winter, stay on the wind-blown ridges to minimize avalanche hazard. (See "Avalanches," page 24.)

Since the access to Rendezvous Peak is on military land and subject to military control, civilian travel may be occasionally restricted. Generally no problems are encountered. Arctic Valley Ski Area buildings and equipment are private property. Please respect them and report any vandalism.

The area is closed to off-road vehicles year-round.

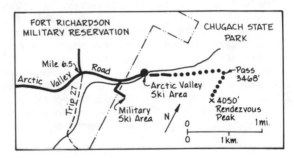

Sliding down the heather on Rendezvous Peak, September (Simmerman photo)

Rendezvous Peak, his first summit (Simmerman photo)

115

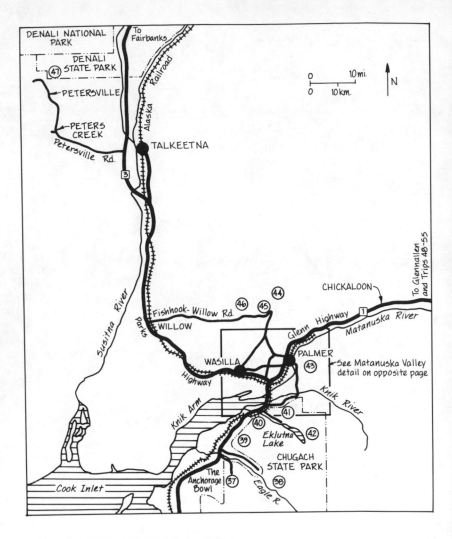

NORTH OF ANCHORAGE

37 Eagle Lake 118
38 The Perch 121
39 Round Top and Black Tail
   Rocks 122
40 Thunder Bird Falls 124
41 East Twin Pass 127
42 Bold Peak Valley 129
43 Lazy Mountain and Matanuska
   Peak 131
44 Reed Lakes 133
45 Hatcher Pass Ski Tour 135
46 Craigie Creek 139
47 Peters Hills 141

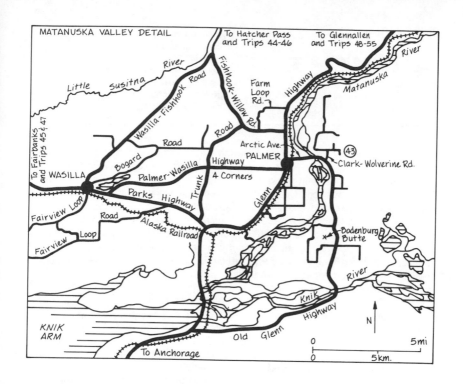

MATANUSKA VALLEY DETAIL

To Hatcher Pass and Trips 44-46

To Glennallen and Trips 48-55

Little Susitna River

Matanuska River

Wasilla-Fishhook Road

Fishhook-Willow Rd.

Farm Loop Rd.

Highway

Road

To Fairbanks and Trips 45 & 47

Bogard Road

Arctic Ave.

PALMER

⊕43

Clark-Wolverine Rd.

WASILLA

Palmer-Wasilla Highway

4 Corners

Glenn

Parks Highway

Trunk

Fairview Loop

Road

Alaska Railroad

Bodenburg Butte

Fairview Loop

River

Knik

KNIK ARM

Old Glenn Highway

N

Knik Highway

To Anchorage

0   5mi
0   5km.

Bull moose (Simmerman photo)

37 Eagle Lake

Round trip 11 miles
Hiking time 6–9 hours
High point 2650 feet
Total elevation gain 750 feet
Best June–early October
USGS map Anchorage A7
Chugach State Park

For a back-country treat, visit shimmering glacier-fed Eagle Lake, then wander through meadows of alpine flowers to nearby clear-water lakes. Beyond lies a wilderness of rugged mountain peaks.

Public access to this scenic valley has long been a problem, resulting in conflicts between landowners and hikers or skiers. Purchase of a bit of real estate by Chugach State Park now provides a legal access to park lands. However, until a parking area and trailhead can be built, public access to this lovely valley will continue to be difficult. Respect private property in the area and do not park on private land. Contact the Chugach State Park office for current access information (address and phone number in the Appendix).

From 6th Avenue and Gambell Street in Anchorage, drive northeast on the Glenn Highway 12 miles to the Hiland Road exit. Immediately turn right onto Hiland Road. (Southbound traffic should cross the freeway overpass on Hiland Road to the east side.) Drive 3.5 miles to the end of state maintenance, take the right-hand fork, and after another 1.5 miles, take another right fork, staying on Hiland Road. After 0.4 mile go left, following Hiland Road downhill and across Throg's Neck bridge. Continue another 1.5 miles, turn right onto South Creek Road. Follow it across the river, turning right onto West River Drive. The Park entrance is on the left (elevation 1900 feet).

Continue on foot. Once clear of private property, follow game trails through light brush, paralleling the South Fork. Head for low ridges on the valley floor. Their crests provide easy walking; the brush thins out farther up the valley. Some boulder-hopping is necessary shortly before Eagle Lake.

From Eagle Lake (elevation 2600 feet), hikes and climbs abound. Symphony Lake (elevation 2645 feet) and the tarns beyond are a fine destination. The ridge between these tarns leads to a high plateau (elevation 4500 feet) overlooking the North Fork of Ship Creek. Challenging peaks in the area, for experienced mountaineers only, include Cantata (elevation 6410 feet), Calliope (elevation 6810 feet) and Eagle Peak (elevation 6955 feet).

A side trip for another day is Eagle River Overlook. From the park entrance, walk

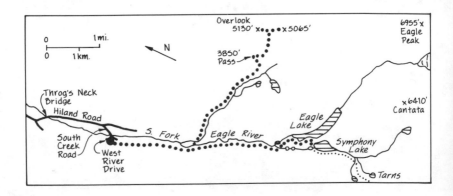

South Fork Eagle River, June (Simmerman photo)

upvalley about 2 miles. To the east, across and at right angles to the South Fork, is a large valley. Cross the South Fork; this may be difficult in high water. (See "Stream crossing," page 18). Climb into this side valley following game trails through brush, staying on the left (north) side of the main drainage.

About 2½ miles from the river climb the steep, grassy slope on the left to a pass at 3850 feet. From here, stroll to points 5065 and 5130 ("Overlook"), both of which provide spectacular views of Eagle River valley and the mountain wilderness beyond. The park entrance to the Overlook is about 13 miles round trip.

Camping is unrestricted on Park lands, but campfires are not permitted; take a stove. Watch for moose, black bears, Dall sheep and mountain goats. Chugach State Park lands in the South Fork drainage are closed to off-road vehicles year-round.

Eagle River near The Perch, November (Simmerman photo)

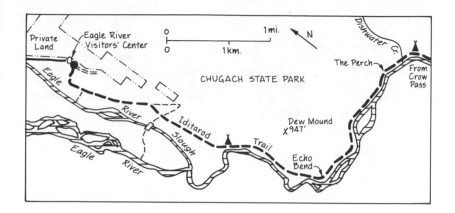

NORTH OF ANCHORAGE

38 The Perch

Round trip 8 miles
Hiking time 4-6 hours
High point 800 feet
Total elevation gain 300 feet
Best May-October
USGS maps Anchorage A6, A7
Chugach State Park

Put a picnic in the your knapsack and stroll to The Perch through a wooded canyon with magnificent mountain scenery all around. This well-maintained trail is a good family hike anytime but is especially nice in early spring or late fall when other hikes are closed by snow. The route lies along the Girdwood to Eagle River part of the historic Iditarod Trail between Seward and the Interior gold fields. (See Trip 25.)

From 6th Ave. and Gambell St. in Anchorage take the Glenn Highway northeast 13.7 miles to the Eagle River exit. Turn right onto the road coming across the overpass. (Southbound traffic should take the second exit for Eagle River, the only one with an overpass, and cross to the east side of the freeway.) Turn right again in 0.1 mile at the traffic light at Eagle River School, onto Eagle River Road. Continue 12.2 miles to the Eagle River Visitors' Center, Chugach State Park.

The trail starts at the Visitors' Center (elevation 500 feet) and is marked as the Iditarod Trail. Check the public information bulletin board before starting on the trail—when bears fish for salmon in streams near the trail, a cautionary notice is posted. Although the trail forks several times, the way is well marked with signs and arrows.

A short side trail 0.3 mile from the Visitors' Center leads to a salmon-viewing stand overlooking Eagle River Slough. At another intersection, about a mile from the trailhead, a 0.6-mile side trail leads to the right, crossing the slough on a bridge, to end at a beaver dam and Eagle River itself.

The main trail wanders through birch and spruce; lichens and mosses cover the rocky ground. The cliffs of Dew Mound are visible to the left. About 2 miles from the Visitors' Center, the trail begins to follow the river closely and, after about 3 miles, reaches a pleasant viewpoint beside the river at Echo Bend. Continue another mile to The Perch (marked), a massive, smooth rock outcropping. With a fine view up the Eagle River canyon to the snowy glaciated peaks beyond, this is the perfect spot for a photo and a sandwich. Another 1½ miles brings you to a view of lovely Heritage Falls, on the south side of Eagle River.

Park personnel request that backpackers use the numerous established campsites available along the trail to reduce the impact on this popular area. Open fires are permitted in park-constructed firepits only. Watch for black bears throughout and for falling dead trees in the burned area.

The trail can be skied in winter when there is enough snow to cover the rocks. After the river freezes, it provides a good alternate route for a ski trip. Check with park rangers for ice conditions, then follow signs to the river from the Visitors' Center.

All trails are closed year-round to off-road vehicles (including snowmobiles and bicycles), horses, and other pack animals.

NORTH OF ANCHORAGE

39 Round Top and Black Tail Rocks

Little Peters Creek access:
Round Top: round trip 10 miles
Black Tail: round trip 12 miles
Hiking time 7-9 hours
High point, Round Top 4755 feet
Total elevation gain, Round Top 4100 feet,
   Black Tail 4510 feet
Best June–September
USGS maps Anchorage B7(NW), B7(SE)

Meadow Creek access:
Black Tail: round trip 8 miles
Round Top: round trip 10 miles
Hiking time 6-8 hours
High point, Round Top 4755 feet
Total elevation gain, Black Tail 2750 feet,
   Round Top 3470 feet
Best June–September
USGS maps Anchorage B7(SW), B7(SE)
Chugach State Park

A panoramic view, from Mt. Redoubt volcano to Denali (Mt. McKinley), rewards the hiker who makes the steep climb to Round Top's summit. All around are the Chugach Mountains, including Bold Peak in the Eklutna area, the high Chugach behind it, and Eagle and Polar Bear peaks in the Eagle River area. This easy day outing takes the urban dweller into a mountain wonderland.

Two approaches are possible: the first via Little Peters Creek, the second via Meadow Creek. The approach up Little Peters Creek will eventually be the official Chugach State Park entrance. The Meadow Creek approach offers the most elevation gain by car, but crosses some private land and requires climbing over Black Tail Rocks to reach Round Top. Call the park office for current access information (phone number in the Appendix).

Little Peters Creek access

From 6th and Gambell in Anchorage, follow the Glenn Highway northeast 21 miles to the exit for North Birchwood and turn right (southbound traffic should cross to the east side of the freeway). In 0.3 mile, turn right onto the Old Glenn Highway. Drive 0.2 mile, then turn left onto Skyline Drive. After 0.25 mile, turn right

Ridge on Round Top, September (Nienhueser photo)

onto Dogwood Drive, then take the first left, Dotberry Drive, and follow it 0.2 mile. Turn right onto Jasmine Street. Park along Jasmine Street well off the road (very limited parking).

Walk up Jasmine Street ⅓ mile to its end (elevation 650 feet). An abandoned road continues up the hill and crosses Little Peters Creek. About 2 miles up this old road, 15-20 minutes beyond the creek and shortly before the road's end, follow an old off-road-vehicle trail that turns left, heading uphill. The ORV trail climbs above the brush before disappearing. From there, climb the tundra-covered slope on the right to a point on Round Top's west ridge. Follow the rocky ridge to a secondary summit for a first view of Round Top, then on to the broad, lichen-covered true summit (elevation 4755 feet).

From Round Top ambitious hikers can follow the ridge to the southeast to Vista Peak (elevation 5070 feet). South and slightly west of Round Top are Black Tail Rocks, which can be reached by following Round Top's southeast ridge, then veering south and west.

Little Peters Creek is the last water. Look for blueberries in early September.

Meadow Creek access

Follow the Glenn Highway 13.6 miles to the Eagle River exit. Turn right onto the road coming across the overpass. (Southbound traffic should take the second exit for Eagle River, the only one with an overpass, and cross to the east side of the freeway.) Continue 0.8 mile on the Old Glenn Highway to Eagle River Loop Road;

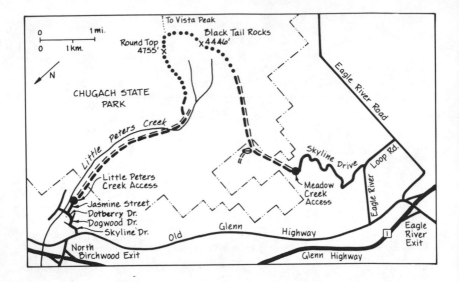

turn right. In 1.1 miles, where the Loop Road bears right, turn left onto Skyline Drive. Drive 2.4 miles to a gate at its end (elevation 1700 feet). (The name of the road changes to Jamie Drive at 0.6 mile.)

On foot, follow the continuing road about a mile. Turn off it to the right onto an old jeep road just before the main road dead-ends at a man-made pond. The old jeep road leads uphill to a broad plateau (elevation 3000-3300 feet). Follow the south edge of the plateau for ¾ mile to Black Tail Rocks (elevation 4446 feet). From here, it is a relatively easy traverse along the ridge to Round Top (elevation 4755 feet) one mile to the north.

Both Round Top and Black Tail Rocks can be climbed in winter, but because of avalanche hazard, use ridge approaches to both and avoid gullies. (See "Avalanches," page 24.) Since the final steep parts may be wind packed, crampons will probably be necessary. The Meadow Creek drainage is open to snowmobiles when snow cover is sufficient. The entire area is closed to off-road vehicles during snow-free months.

NORTH OF ANCHORAGE

40 Thunder Bird Falls

Round trip 2 miles
Hiking time 1 hour
High point 330 feet
Total elevation gain 200 feet in, 130 feet out
Best May–October
USGS map Anchorage B7(NE)
Chugach State Park

A pleasant outing for families with small children, this trail leads through woods to a rushing stream and a view of a pretty waterfall. Though snow patches linger deep in the gorge near the falls well into May, the walk is good any time snow cover permits. Under the birch trees, the forest floor is laced with wild roses and ferns.

Along the trail, children can learn to recognize and stay away from devil's club, a prickly, large-leafed shrub up to 6 feet high.

From Anchorage, drive northeast on the Glenn Highway to mile 25.2, Thunder Bird Falls exit, and drive 0.4 mile to a parking area on the right, just before the Eklutna River bridge. The trailhead (elevation 130 feet) is marked. (Southbound traffic should exit at Eklutna, mile 26, Glenn Highway, cross the bridge over the freeway to the east side and turn right onto the Old Glenn Highway. Drive 0.6 mile to the trailhead parking area on the left.)

An inviting broad trail leads 1 mile to Thunder Bird Creek and the falls. The trail can be dusty during dry weather and slick during wet. Near the end, just as you begin to hear the sound of the falls, the trail forks. Both forks go steeply downhill to the stream, but the right-hand one provides the more gradual descent.

As the falls cannot be seen when you reach the stream, they are an extra dividend when you find them. A trail leads upstream about 100 yards toward the falls, which are hidden in the back of a narrow gorge. The sun reaches here only a few hours a day. Do not go beyond the end of the foot path and do not allow children to explore the cliffs, where they would be in danger of falling. Several deaths have occurred in this manner.

Thunder Bird Falls, September (Nienhueser photo)

Trail to Thunder Bird Falls, May (Nienhueser photo)

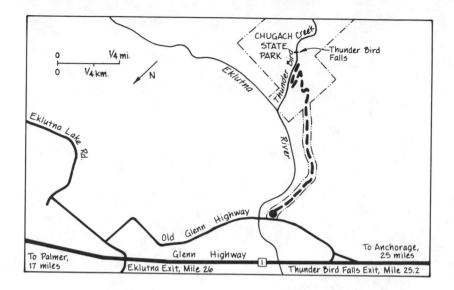

This long-time favorite trail has lost some of its charm because it now passes near a subdivision on a 25-foot-wide easement. Houses are visible from the trail, though not from the falls.

To reach the southbound (Anchorage) freeway lane from the Thunder Bird Falls parking area, drive 0.6 mile north on the Old Glenn Highway, crossing the Eklutna River bridge. Follow freeway entrance signs. Northbound traffic should drive south from the trailhead parking area to the freeway entrance.

The trail is closed to off-road vehicles year-round.

NORTH OF ANCHORAGE

41 East Twin Pass

Round trip 9 miles
Hiking time 6–8 hours
High point 5050 feet
Total elevation gain 4150 feet
Best July–September
USGS map Anchorage B6
Chugach State Park

Follow an abandoned road to timberline and continue up alpine tundra to a magnificent view. Aqua Eklutna Lake lies southward far below, while to the north spreads a vast panorama of the Matanuska Valley. With the Twin Peaks always in view during the ascent, the hike is mysterious on gray days when clouds swirl around the summits. Chances of seeing Dall sheep are good.

Drive northeast from Anchorage on the Glenn Highway to mile 26, the Eklutna exit. Turn right onto the road coming across the overpass. (Southbound traffic should cross the overpass to the east side of the freeway.) Turn immediately left onto the frontage road and go 0.5 mile. (See map, Trip 40.) Turn right at a "T" intersection, passing a sign for Eklutna Lake. Follow this road about 9½ miles to its end

Eklutna Lake from Twin Peaks trail, September (Simmerman photo)

at the lake and Eklutna Lake Campground, and park (elevation 900 feet). The first 3 miles of the road are steep and winding.

From the northeast side of the parking area loop, walk across a short bridge to the picnic area. Bear left to the Twin Peaks trailhead (marked). Bear left again, following trail signs until a well-defined trail begins to climb the hillside.

About ¼ mile from the campground, the trail forks. Both forks rejoin in about ½ mile: the right-hand trail climbs with a switchback; the left fork is a shorter but steeper route. As you climb, enjoy the fine views of the lake behind you and of Twin Peaks to the north.

Brushline, at about 2700 feet, 2½ –3 hours round trip, may be destination enough. A sparkling stream rushes through a small canyon in the alpine bowl above; camping or picnicking is tempting. The first water along the trail is available at the stream, a short distance through high grass below the road.

To continue to the pass, head diagonally down through the grass to the stream. A trail of sorts leads from the end of the road to the first draw coming down from the

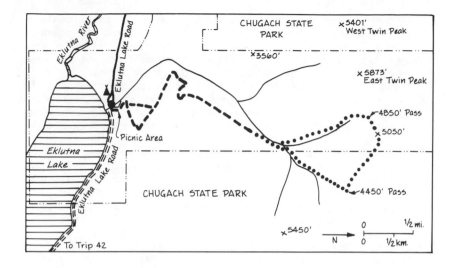

peak to the northeast. If you lose the trail, work your way to the stream and head for the low 4450-foot pass to the northeast. High grass is soon left behind. For the best Matanuska Valley vistas, follow the ridge crest northwest to the 5050-foot knob. To make a circular route, continue west to the 4850-foot pass and then down the steep south slope, staying west of the stream below the pass.

Climbing either of the peaks requires experience and mountaineering equipment. The usual approach to East Twin is from the 4850-foot pass.

The trail is closed to off-road vehicles year-round.

NORTH OF ANCHORAGE

42 Bold Peak Valley

Round trip 16 miles
Hiking time 9–12 hours
High point 3400 feet
Total elevation gain 2500 feet
Best late June–early October
USGS map Anchorage B6
Chugach State Park

The hike to Bold Peak valley, good any time, is unsurpassed in September, when Bold Peak is topped with white, the alpine valley is carpeted in red, the lower hillsides are sheathed in gold, and Eklutna lake, far below, is a lovely aqua. Watch for moose, parka squirrels, magpies, Dall sheep, mountain goats and, in season, beautiful wildflowers, high-bush cranberries, and blueberries.

Drive northeast from Anchorage on the Glenn Highway to mile 26, the Eklutna exit. Turn right, onto the road coming across the overpass. (Southbound traffic should cross the overpass to the east side of the freeway.) Turn immediately left onto the frontage road and go 0.5 mile. (See map, Trip 40.) Turn right at a "T" intersection, passing a sign for Eklutna Lake. Follow this road about 9½ miles to its end at the Eklutna Lake Campground and park (elevation 900 feet). The first 3 miles of the road are steep and winding.

From the northeast side of the parking area loop, walk across a short bridge to the picnic area. (See map, Trip 41.) Turn right and follow the road around the left side of the lake 5½ miles to a large stream that goes under the road through four large culverts. Cross it, go 150 yards, and turn sharply left onto an old road. The trail (marked) begins 50 yards north of this junction. Bicycles can be ridden to the trailhead.

Ignoring side trails, follow the trail as it climbs steeply through timber to brushline (about 2500 feet). The trail disappears in another mile (about 3400 feet). Note that the stream which USGS maps show draining the valley flows partly underground, limiting access to drinking water. At the head of the valley, near the gravel moraine, the stream runs on the surface. It then goes underground and does not reappear until it is north of point 3465. Good campsites can be found near the stream.

From the end of the trail a variety of hikes beckon. For magnificent views of Bold Peak (elevation 7522 feet), Eklutna Lake and Glacier, and surrounding mountains, climb the ridge to the south. On top, walk the heights 1 mile to point 4456.

For a 6-mile loop, walk to the head of the valley, climb to Hunter Creek Pass (elevation 4850 feet), then up to point 5281. There are good views of the relatively inaccessible Hunter Creek valley and the mountain wilderness rising behind it. Follow point 5281's northwest ridge back to the trail. Bold Peak should be attempted only by experienced climbers.

Bold Peak from Eklutna Lake, September (Simmerman photo)

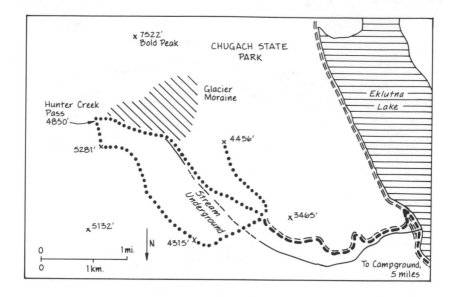

The road leading around the lake from the Eklutna Lake Campground is closed by washouts; however, it may be reopened someday. Until then, motorized all-terrain vehicles are permitted on the road surface only, Wednesdays through Saturdays; all other areas are closed to off-road vehicles. Small powerboats are permitted on Eklutna Lake. No boat ramp exists; boats must be carried from the parking area. Contact the Chugach State Park office (address and phone number in the Appendix) for further information.

NORTH OF ANCHORAGE

43 Lazy Mountain and Matanuska Peak

Round trip 5 miles
Hiking time 5–6 hours
High point 3720 feet
Total elevation gain 3120 feet
Best May–October
USGS map Anchorage C6

The steep but pleasant hike up Lazy Mountain leads to a craggy summit with a glorious view. Children as young as 4 years have made the climb . But of course, they take additional time. The return trip downhill is especially good for running, jumping, and sliding. Matanuska Peak lies 4 miles beyond Lazy Mountain's summit and 2399 feet higher.

The Matanuska Valley, a fertile farming center, spreads out below the peaks. To the northeast the upper valley becomes pinched between the Chugach and Talkeetna mountain ranges. To the south, Knik and Matanuska rivers join to flow into Knik Arm. Pioneer Peak soars majestically above the Knik River, while nearby Bodenburg Butte shows clearly as a knob west of the Old Glenn Highway.

Reach the trailhead, from mile 42.1, Glenn Highway (42 miles northeast of Anchorage and the third turnoff for Palmer). Turn east onto Arctic Avenue, which is

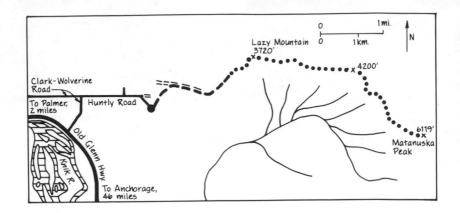

easily identified by a Tesoro station on the corner. Drive 2.3 miles, crossing the Matanuska River, to Clark-Wolverine Road (marked). Turn left, continue 0.6 mile to a "T" junction, and turn right onto Huntly Road (not marked). Drive 1 mile to the crest of the hill and a "Y" intersection. Follow the right-hand fork downhill 0.2 mile to a parking area and a small building (elevation 600 feet).

The trail, marked only with a "Foot Trail" sign, begins at the left (north) side of the parking area. After about 100 yards, at a fork, take the right-hand trail. It joins an

Matanuska Valley view from Lazy Mountain, July (Nienhueser photo)

overgrown jeep track, which soon becomes a trail that is well defined all the way to brushline.

The lower portion of the trail winds through low brush and tall grass, which may be wet with raindrops, dew, or frost even on a clear day. So take along a pair of rain pants and wear well-greased boots. The path becomes quite steep and, in spots, may be muddy and slippery. Beyond the first of several false summits, where the growth gives way to low berry bushes, the grade becomes gentler. From here, pick your own route up the tundra-covered slopes. The last 200 feet of Lazy Mountain's summit ridge are narrow and exposed; children will need help. The route crosses no streams for drinking water.

Wildflowers abound; new species of flowers introduce themselves with every hundred feet of elevation gained, culminating on the ridge crest in minute lichens, with brilliant pinhead-sized sporangia, clinging to the rocks.

Energetic hikers may want to continue on to Matanuska Peak (elevation 6119 feet), the real mountain, looming 4 miles to the east of Lazy Mountain. The route is generally free of snow by July. The hike is a long one—12-14 hours round trip from the trailhead—but about half the total elevation is gained by the time you reach the summit of Lazy Mountain. Much of what remains is a long undulating ridge walk, culminating in rock scrambling. At the end of the long ridge between Lazy Mountain and Matanuska Peak, head to the right up the northwest ridge of Matanuska Peak. From the top of this ridge, approach the summit rock pile up a loose scree slope. Go right at the final rocks. A rope belay is not necessary if the route is carefully chosen. Because of the length of this hike, consider taking flashlights on all but the longest days of summer. The summit usually has snow until July.

NORTH OF ANCHORAGE

44 Reed Lakes

Round trip, Lower Reed Lake 7 miles;
Upper Reed Lake 9 miles
Hiking time 5-7 hours
High point 4250 feet
Total elevation gain 1850 feet
Best July–September
USGS map Anchorage D6

Under towering granite spires reminiscent of the High Sierra, plunging cascades feed Reed Lakes. Located at the edge of the vast wilderness of the Talkeetna Mountains, this alpine world is unlike any other near Anchorage. Watch for ptarmigan, marmots, parka squirrels, pikas, northern shrikes and eagles.

Reach the trailhead from mile 35.3, Glenn Highway (35 miles northeast of Anchorage) by turning west onto the Parks Highway. In 0.4 mile, turn right onto Trunk Road, drive 6.5 miles, then turn left and follow the Fishhook-Willow Road. (See area map, page 116.) About 11½ miles from Trunk Road, the road leaves the scenic gorge of the Little Susitna River, making a sharp switchback to the left around a roadhouse. A mile farther, turn sharply right onto the road to Fern Mine. (The Fishhook-Willow Road continues to Hatcher Pass.) Drive 2.5 miles and turn right at a side road (not marked) leading to the old Snowbird Mine "village." Park here (elevation 2400 feet).

To reach Reed Lakes, walk the eroded, nearly overgrown Snowbird Mine road 1½ miles to its end at a privately owned house and the ruins of the abandoned Snowbird Mine "village" (elevation 2700 feet). Lower Reed Lake is 2 miles away, Upper

Pool en route to Lower Reed Lake (Nienhueser photo)

Reed Lake, a mile farther. The hanging valley of Glacier Creek to the northwest is a nice side trip.

Reed Creek valley is not obvious from the mine buildings. The creek comes down from the middle valley north of the "village"; look for cascades part way up it. From the wooden frame house, follow a trail to the first stream, Glacier Creek, and cross on a bridge. About 300 feet farther, through tall grass, cross Reed Creek on large granite boulders beside a partly submerged pipe. At high water, wading may be necessary, or bushwhack along the left stream bank.

After crossing Reed Creek, find the trail through the grass. (Note where you crossed the stream so you don't miss the spot on the return trip.) The trail climbs steeply up a hill, then contours left below the hilltop to an area covered by large granite boulders. Boulder-hopping is necessary here, a difficult route for less-agile hikers, young children, and dogs. Beyond the boulder field, follow sparkling Reed Creek through grassy meadows and past small, clear pools that reflect the surrounding mountains. At these pools cross to the north side of the creek and climb 200 feet to the aqua beauty of Lower Reed Lake (elevation 3750 feet). Stay high on the left

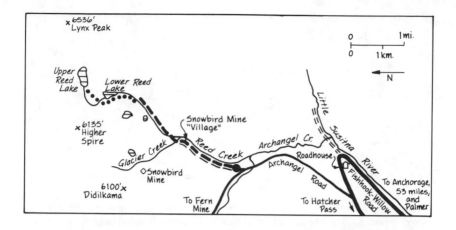

above the stream. Above the lake, a lovely waterfall cascades over rock slabs.

To reach Upper Reed Lake (elevation 4250 feet), a mile from the lower lake, skirt left of the falls, crossing rocks and grassy meadows. Beyond a shallow lakelet, vivid-aqua Upper Reed Lake appears. It is larger than the lower lake and set in a cirque at the base of Lynx Peak (elevation 6536 feet). Granite spires and sheer faces rise high above talus and glaciers. The lakes are often ice-covered into July.

Many good campsites are available, from just beyond the boulder field to the mossy hummocks at Upper Reed Lake. No firewood is available in this alpine area; bring a stove for cooking. Hardy types swim in the chilly waters.

The trip from the Fishhook-Willow Road to Snowbird Mine "village" is a good winter ski or snowshoe tour over gently sloping terrain. Take a shovel to dig out a place to park off the road. Snowmobiles use the area.

NORTH OF ANCHORAGE

45 Hatcher Pass Ski Tour

One-way trip 14 miles
Skiing time 5–8 hours
High point 3886 feet
Total elevation gain 950 feet
Best December–April
USGS maps Anchorage D7, D8

The unplowed portion of the Fishhook-Willow Road provides a beautiful ski tour through the Talkeetna Mountains. A 1½-mile climb with an elevation gain of 950 feet places the skier at Hatcher Pass. From there it is all downhill for 12½ miles, an elevation loss of about 2300 feet. The route follows the unplowed Fishhook-Willow Road. The brush-free slopes of mountains garbed in winter finery are excellent for telemarking. Nearby valleys invite exploration.

A major flaw in this rosy picture is the 2-hour drive between the ends of the trail. Arrange to be picked up at the Willow end of the trail if possible. The ski trip over the pass is more pleasant on a weekday since snowmobilers often hold weekend races in January and February.

Reach the trailhead from mile 35.3, Glenn Highway (35 miles northeast of An-

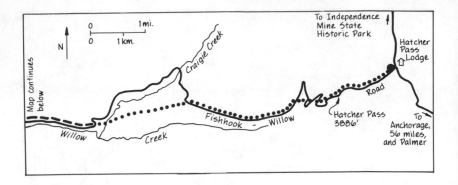

chorage) by turning left onto the Parks Highway. In 0.4 mile, turn right onto Trunk Road, drive 6.5 miles, and turn left onto Fishhook-Willow Road. (See area map, page 116.) Drive 15 miles, passing through the scenic gorge of the Little Susitna River and switching back around a roadhouse. The road is steep, narrow, and winding. Studded winter tires are mandatory and chains may be necessary. At the A-frames of the Hatcher Pass Lodge, 3.5 miles beyond the roadhouse, park in an area provided. A side road is plowed a mile farther, to Independence Mine State Historic Park.

Ski west up the slope leading to Hatcher Pass. Road switchbacks should be visible to guide you. Snowmobiles generally pack the snow on this side of the pass, less so on the west side. At Hatcher Pass the long downhill begins. Finding the route is no problem as the drainage pattern is distinct and leads naturally along Willow Creek and the unplowed road. Note the old mine buildings high on the slopes to the right near Craigie Creek.

From the Willow end, the road is plowed for about 17 miles, to 2 miles east of the bridge. This makes a good destination, though some may prefer to ski the remaining distance to Willow. Alaska Railroad trains pass through Willow on a limited winter schedule, giving skiers the option of returning to Anchorage by train. Check with the railroad office for schedule and pick-up point (address and phone number in the Appendix).

Rather than crossing Hatcher Pass, skiers can spend a pleasant day touring in the Independence Mine bowl north of the Hatcher Pass Lodge. The lodge and Ski Touring Center offer meals, bar, lodging and groomed ski trails. Those using the groomed trails are expected to pay a small fee for the privilege. Check at the lodge for information on snow and avalanche conditions. (See "Avalanches," page 24.) The State Park visitors' center is open on weekends on a limited schedule.

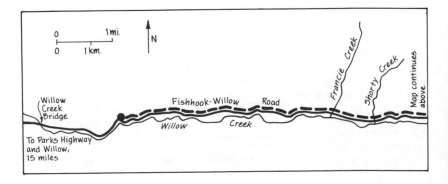

En route to Hatcher Pass, November (Simmerman photo)

Independence Mine buildings in 1970 (Simmerman photo)

The weather in Hatcher Pass, though often still and warm, is unpredictable. Even on the clearest of days, wind gusts can cause settled snow to swirl up in great clouds to create "ground blizzards." Temperatures are generally colder than in Anchorage. Take extra warm clothes and a flashlight with strong batteries. In mid-winter, daylight lasts only from 9:30 a.m. to 4 p.m.

To reach the Willow end of the trail from the Independence Mine area, drive 10.5 miles back down Fishhook-Willow Road toward Palmer. Turn right onto the Wasilla-Fishhook Road, the second road to the right after leaving the mountains, marked "Wasilla 11" (miles). At Wasilla, turn right onto the Parks Highway and drive 29 miles to mile 71.2, the junction with the Fishhook-Willow Road. Turn right and drive about 17 miles to the end of the plowed road. To reach Willow from Anchorage (71 miles), drive the Glenn Highway 35 miles to the Parks Highway; follow the Parks Highway to Willow.

46 Craigie Creek

Round trip 3 miles
Hiking time 2–4 hours
High point 4250 feet
Total elevation gain 950 feet
Best late July–early October
USGS map Anchorage D7

Take a picnic lunch to a blue-green alpine lake at the base of precipitous peaks and spires. The short walk is just right for families with children, but don't overlook this charming hike to Dogsled Pass as an entrance to outstanding wilderness hiking deep into the Talkeetna Mountains. For less active explorers the scenic summer drive over Hatcher Pass is a fine excursion in itself.

Reach Craigie Creek from mile 35.3, Glenn Highway (35 miles northeast of Anchorage) by turning west onto the Parks Highway. In 0.4 mile, turn right onto Trunk Road, drive 6.5 miles, and turn left onto Fishhook-Willow Road. (See area map, page 116. Fishhook-Willow Road, which goes over Hatcher Pass, is narrow, steep, and winding, unsafe for trailers and large camper vehicles.) Drive 16 miles, through the scenic gorge of the Little Susitna River and past the side road to Independence Mine State Historic Park. Continue over Hatcher Pass. About 3 miles west of the pass, the road forks; take the left fork. Continue another 3.5 miles to a side road turning right into the valley of Craigie Creek. Because of deep snow, the road does not open until mid-June and then it may be wet, soft, and rough.

At the beginning of the Craigie Creek road, note the entrances of Lucky Shot and War Baby mines high on the mountains to the left. Gold mining in the Craigie Creek area began prior to 1919 and continued at least through 1930. It gradually died out as inflation made mining uneconomical. With the increase in the price of gold, mining activities have begun again. If areas are posted against trespassing, respect the signs. The route may cross private property, although hikers have used this access for years without complications. In any case, do not disturb buildings or equipment, nor remove rocks or other minerals. Should you meet a miner, ask permission to continue hiking.

The Craigie Creek road is rough and not maintained. If it is dry, cars with high clearance may be able to drive almost 3 miles; park well off the road. One possible parking spot (elevation 3300 feet) is on the right, where the ruins of a cabin can be seen across the creek (about 2.8 miles from the main road). Beyond there the road will probably be worse.

On foot, continue on the road as it climbs gently, passing old buildings and then waterfalls. The road then becomes a foot trail leading to Dogsled Pass (elevation

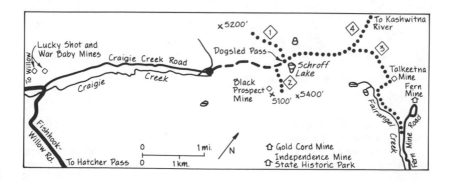

Schroff Lake, Dogsled Pass, July (Nienhueser photo)

4250 feet), high above timberline, and a lovely tarn locally known as Schroff Lake. The north side of the pass is covered by acres of granite boulders.

Hikes and climbs abound. (1) From Dogsled Pass, an easy walk leads up the west ridge to several high points. (2) A rock scramble up the gully next to Black Prospect

Mine entrance brings you to the ridge crest and a view of the historic Independence Mine buildings far below. (3) From Dogsled Pass, bear right across the flats and climb over a 5150-foot pass to the high valley containing Talkeetna Mine. Descend to Fairangel Creek and follow it to the Fern Mine road. (See Trip 44.) (4) From Dogsled Pass, head north through a vast area of alpine lakes and 6000- foot peaks to the Kashwitna River drainage.

In winter the Fishhook-Willow Road over Hatcher Pass is not plowed between the Hatcher Pass Lodge (Independence Mine area) and the Willow Creek bridge.

NORTH OF ANCHORAGE

47 Peters Hills

Round trip 4–14 miles
Allow 3 hours to 2 days
High point 2840 or 3929 feet
Total elevation gain 1000–2480 feet
Best July–September
USGS map Talkeetna C2
Denali State Park

The majestic white presence of Denali (Mt. McKinley) dominates the skyline 40 miles north of the Peters Hills. While the view from point 2840, 2 miles from the trailhead, is excellent, the vista up the Tokositna Glacier from Long Point at the eastern end of the ridge is breathtaking. Famed Alaskan artist Sydney Laurence painted many of his pictures of Denali from just below Long Point.

Excellent camping beside small alpine lakes dotting the ridge make this a good backpacking trip for families with children. Look for blueberries and lingonberries in season and watch for brown (grizzly) bears. The hike is particularly scenic in early September, when the rich reds and golds of autumn foliage are at their best. Unfortunately, the area is also popular with hunters, particularly on weekends.

At mile 114.8, Parks Highway (115 miles north of Anchorage), turn west onto the Petersville Road, a homestead and mining access marked "Peters Creek 19" (miles). Peters Hills are 31 miles away. To Peters Creek and the Forks Roadhouse the road is fairly good gravel. Turn right at the roadhouse. From this point the road

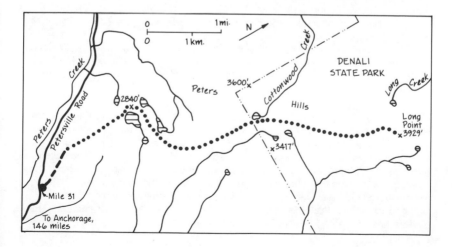

Denali (Mt. McKinley) from Peters Hills, September (Simmerman photo)

narrows, is poorly maintained, and may have deep mudholes during break-up. When the road is dry, usually by July, cars with sufficient clearance can reach the trailhead. Allow 4-5 hours to drive the 146 miles from Anchorage. (Contact the Alaska Department of Transportation for a road condition report; its phone number is in the Appendix.)

About 11 miles north of the Forks Roadhouse, watch for the tailing piles and buildings of the Petersville placer mine. Drive 1 mile farther and look for a tracked-vehicle trail leaving the right-hand side of the road. Park well off the road (elevation 1825 feet).

The first viewpoint is 2 miles away. Follow the tracked- vehicle trail uphill through brush, bearing left (northwest) toward a dry ridge and easier walking. An eastward-bound, off-road-vehicle trail does not climb the ridge. Continue up the approach ridge to a fine view of Denali and the Alaska Range from point 2840, an obvious high point.

Long Point (elevation 3929 feet) is 5 miles away. Hike along the tundra-covered ridge as far as time permits. Sunlight, clouds, and storms sweeping through the mountain panorama to the north are hypnotizing. Watch the sunset, the sunrise and the northern lights play with the continent's highest peak and its consorts.

Camp anywhere. Water is easily available, but take a stove for cooking. The eastern half of the ridge lies in Denali State Park.

Right: *Monarch Peak in the Talkeetna Mountains—Trip 48 (Nienhueser photo)*

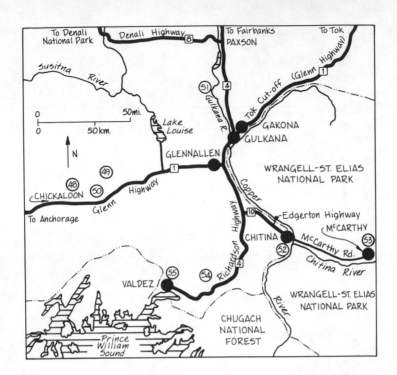

CHICKALOON TO VALDEZ

48 Hicks Creek/Chitna Pass 145
49 Syncline Mountain 148
50 Gunsight Mountain in Winter . . 152
51 Gulkana River 154
52 Chitina Railroad Bed 157
53 Kennecott Mines 159
54 Worthington Glacier Overlook . 161
55 Mineral Creek Valley 163

48 Hicks Creek/ Chitna Pass

One-way trip 42 miles
Allow 4–5 days
High point 4700 feet
Total elevation gain 4120 feet eastbound,
   3680 feet westbound
Best late June–September
USGS maps Anchorage D2, D3, D4
Matanuska Valley Moose Range

The Talkeetna Mountains, which invite endless wandering, are a fascinating wilderness of peaks, tundra, alpine valleys, and clear mountain streams, many of them far from civilization. A nearly circular route is described. By using this trip as an access, many other trips, limited primarily by your time and food supply, can be planned from topographic maps.

According to old-timers, prospectors traveled on this trail in the early 1900s. The route took them from Knik (which in summer could be reached by boat from Seattle) and Chickaloon, up Boulder Creek, over Chitna Pass, and along Caribou Creek to Alfred Creek (Trip 49). Their destinations were gold prospects and mines on Alfred and Albert creeks. Trips 48 and 49 can be combined in several ways, although Caribou Creek may be difficult to cross downstream from Divide Creek.

Route to Chitna Pass, August (Simmerman photo)

Crossing Boulder Creek channel, August (Simmerman photo)

The route described here is not a marked, maintained trail but rather a collection of off-road-vehicle (ORV), horse, and game trails. The trip is not for novices because help may be far away. Experienced backpackers, in good condition and able to follow USGS maps, will find this a delightful experience. Though lovely in the rich autumn colors of early September, this country is then invaded by hunters; hikers seeking quiet solitude will want to plan their trip earlier in the summer. Watch for moose, black bears, brown (grizzly) bears, Dall sheep, wolves, and coyotes.

A westbound trip is described primarily because the unsightly scars of ORV use are soon passed and out of mind; on a clear day the approach to the western trailhead at the end of the trip is unforgettable.

From mile 99.2, Glenn Highway (99 miles northeast of Anchorage), opposite powerline pole no. 7746, turn north onto a dirt road. Park here (elevation 1776 feet), without blocking the road, or park south of the highway. The first section of the trail is known locally as either the Pinochle Creek Trail or the Hicks Creek Trail.

On foot, follow the dirt road north. It quickly becomes an ORV trail that climbs above timberline to a 3150-foot pass. The trail is deeply rutted and often mucky, an example of what mechanized transportation does to wet tundra country. Thought-less visitors have also left much litter, but the total trip is worth this initial visual discomfort.

From the pass, the trail descends to Hicks Creek at 3000 feet. A side trip heads

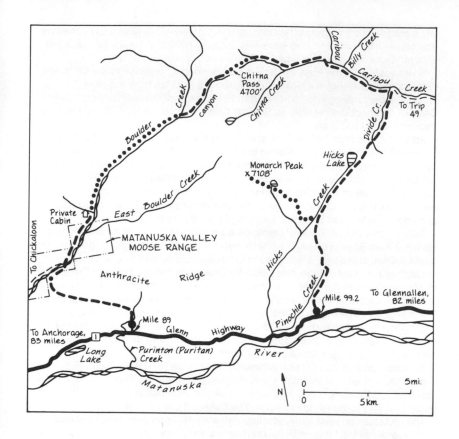

northwest across Hicks Creek to a small alpine lake (elevation 5000 feet), about 5 miles away (good camping, but no firewood). Monarch Peak (elevation 7108 feet), towering above the lake, is the highest in the area and a steep but easy climb.

The main trail continues to Hicks Lake, with a good campsite at the south end. High tundra all around tempts further exploration. Watch for muskrats in the lake, ptarmigan and parka squirrels on the tundra. Beyond Hicks Lake the ORV trail crosses a low 3300-foot pass, then follows a small stream down to Caribou Creek (elevation 2800 feet), about 4 miles from Hicks Lake.

Follow the trail up the south side of Caribou Creek, passing many good campsites. Look for agate, jasper, and other brightly- colored stones. Just above the junction with Billy Creek, climb the bank to avoid cliffs and travel the bluff until the route below is clear. Do not cross Caribou Creek at any point; the trail shown on the USGS map as running along the north side of the creek does not exist.

Above the junction of Chitna and Caribou creeks, the trail follows the south bank of Chitna Creek a short distance, then drops to the stream and a good campsite. Cross the creek and climb the opposite bank. Chitna Creek is swift, but not deep nor difficult to cross.

The trail now blends with game trails, making it difficult to follow; but it does continue to Chitna Pass and is therefore worth the search. About 2½ miles from Caribou Creek, turn northwest up a tributary of Chitna Creek toward Chitna Pass. At 3600 feet the vegetation changes from brush to open tundra—and delightful walking. A gradual climb to Chitna Pass (elevation 4700 feet)—2½ miles away—leads to fine country for camping and exploring. Nearby 6000-foot peaks can be easily climbed. Drinking water is available, but firewood is not.

Southwest of Chitna Pass the trail is well defined as it parallels a small creek. Where the stream enters a small canyon, about 2½ miles from the pass, the trail stays on a descending ridge northwest of the canyon all the way down to Boulder Creek. It does not drop steeply to Boulder Creek directly west of Chitna Pass, as shown on the USGS map.

About 4 miles from Chitna Pass the well-defined trail ends where it enters the Boulder Creek gravel bars. Following the southeast river bank requires scrambling over bluffs, necessary perhaps if Boulder Creek is in flood and cannot be easily crossed. If the water level is low and you don't mind wet feet, walking the river bed, splashing across the braided channels, is the easiest way to continue. At higher water, cross Boulder Creek once, and stay on the northwest side where occasional stretches of a trail can be found. Camping is good on the river bar.

About 7 miles down Boulder Creek, on its west side, and shortly before the entrance of East Boulder Creek, is a private cabin. From this point, walking is easy on a well-defined horse trail, which goes to Chickaloon. However, just before reaching the bluff of Anthracite Ridge, cross Boulder Creek and find the Purinton Creek Trail on the east bank of the stream, at the base of the ridge. On some maps it may be labeled the Chickaloon-Knik-Nelchina Trail. Follow this trail south, then east to the Glenn Highway. The trail has a few boggy spots, but generally the walking is good. Little water is available; there are few desirable campsites. On a clear day the approach to the Purinton Creek trailhead is spectacular, with its panoramic view to the south of the rugged Chugach Mountains.

To reach the Purinton Creek trailhead by road, drive to mile 89, Glenn Highway. About 100 feet east of Purinton Creek (highway sign reads "Puritan Creek") is a short dirt road heading north, then east. Follow the road, parking where an ORV trail ascends a very steep hill to the north. The trailhead elevation is 2200 feet.

The route can be used for ski touring, either as day trips from either trailhead or as a several-day trip for experienced ski tourers and winter campers. The route near the trailheads is likely to be packed by snowmobiles. In midwinter prepare for very cold weather as temperatures to −30° F are not uncommon.

CHICKALOON TO VALDEZ

49 Syncline Mountain

Traverse or round trip 25 miles
Allow 3 days
High point 5471 feet
Total elevation gain: traverse over summit 4400 feet, round trip 3800 feet
Best June–September
USGS maps Anchorage D1, D2

The routes described here provide access into the back country of the Talkeetna Mountains, which are inhabited primarily by caribou, sheep, miners, and—during the last part of the summer—hunters. Part of the trip lies along the route of the old Chickaloon-Knik-Nelchina Trail, which provided access to gold mines on Alfred and Albert creeks before there was a Glenn Highway. Several different trips are possible, including a climb of Syncline Mountain and a traverse around the mountain. The climb is not difficult, offers nice views of the Chugach and Talkeetna moun-

Campsite overlooking Caribou Creek, July (Nienhueser photo)

tains, avoids most of the mining, and the hiker is more likely to see sheep and caribou. On either trip look also for ptarmigan, parka squirrels, rabbits, porcupines, water ouzels, hawks, moose, black bears, brown (grizzly) bears, coyotes, and wolves. In season there are blueberries and the gamut of Alaskan wildflowers.

The traverse follows the valleys of Squaw, Caribou, Alfred, and Pass creeks, then over Belanger Pass, in a circular trip around Syncline Mountain. Off-road-vehicle (ORV) trails can be followed in places, but elsewhere hikers must search for game trails. Hiking time averages about 1 mile per hour in this terrain. In the early 1900s the Alfred Creek part of the route was traveled by prospectors coming from Knik Arm by way of Chitna Pass (see Trip 48). Gold was discovered on Alfred Creek in 1911, but prospectors were also going beyond Alfred to Albert and Crooked Creeks. When the price of gold was deregulated in the mid-1970s, mining activity began again and has affected both Squaw Creek and Alfred Creek valleys.

For either trip start at Squaw Creek. Park in the gravel pit at mile 117.6, Glenn Highway, opposite powerline pole no. 7151 (elevation 3350 feet). A sign, "Squaw Creek trail," marks the beginning of the ORV trail (locally known as Meekin's trail); follow it north over the toe (elevation 3600 feet) of Gunsight Mountain and down into the valley of Squaw Creek at 2700 feet, a distance of about 3 miles. In places this trail is very wet. Those who take more than 3 days will find beautiful camping in another mile in spruce woods just across Gunsight Creek.

From here either follow the ORV trail through a swampy area or stay in the spruce woods and parallel Squaw Creek for a little less than a mile. Then cross the stream (no problem normally—about a foot deep) and head straight uphill to a dirt road.

Caribou, September (Simmerman photo)

Follow this road west about 2 miles and look for an old ORV trail overgrown with grass (about 400 yards before the road crosses Squaw Creek). Follow this uphill and left (west) through brush until it peters out.

Continue cross-country, heading for the pass between two bumps (locally known as Twin Peaks) which separate Squaw Creek valley from Caribou Creek valley. From here to Alfred Creek there is no trail, but usually a game trail can be found through the brush. Stay high (elevation about 3200 feet) while contouring around northern Twin Peak and begin looking for a campsite. Some streams on this east slope are underground in spots so listen for water. The only wood generally available is scrub willow. Total first-day distance is about 9 miles.

From this point you can head for the summit (1) of Syncline Mountain (elevation 5471 feet) or continue contouring (2) around the mountain toward Alfred Creek. To climb the mountain, head up the southwest ridge. Game trails make much of the route easy, and the ridge-top walking is delightful. From the suggested camping area to the high point at 5471 feet is a little over 2 miles. From point 5471 a number of trips are possible. Stay high, exploring ridges and watching wildlife, returning at day's end to camp. Or descend via the steep north ridge (3) toward the plateau above Alfred Creek and continue the traverse around Syncline Mountain. Camp just above the plateau. This requires 4 days or an extremely long 3rd day. Another possibility is to follow the ridgetops (4) east and north to Belanger Pass, about 7 miles.

Those traversing around the mountain will also find game trails to help them. Near the base of the northwest side of Syncline Mountain a plateau at about 3150 feet elevation overlooks Alfred Creek. Here pick up a mining road that cuts across the plateau and leads to a mining operation near the confluence of Sawmill and Alfred creeks (elevation 2900 feet). Avoid the mine buildings, which are private property, and continue up Alfred Creek. An ORV trail cuts back and forth across Alfred Creek. Cross the stream at the first wide place as it becomes increasingly difficult upstream. Cliffs on the south bank make this route impassable. This is a potentially dangerous stream as it is at least knee-deep and very swift.

On the north side follow the ORV trail where possible and bushwhack or follow

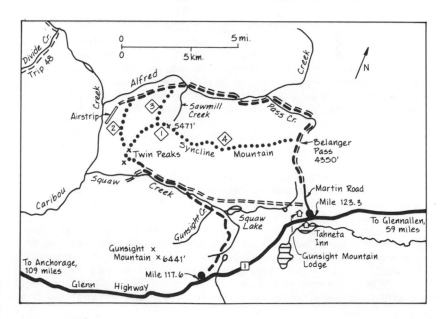

gravel bars where there is no trail. This whole stretch has been thoroughly disturbed by recent mining. Once past the cliffs (about 2 miles downstream from Pass Creek) recross the stream. This crossing is easier, and an ORV trail continues on the south side to Pass Creek. Hikers who camp near Pass Creek the second night will have an easy last day. However, finding a campsite out of sight of the mining scars may be difficult. Total second-day distance about 9 miles.

Pass Creek should be easy to find as a tractor trail leads up to it. Look for a stream that comes from a broad pass (Belanger Pass). In early summer ice may cover the trail beginning so that it is not obvious.

From the junction of Pass and Alfred creeks (elevation 3400 feet) to the Glenn Highway, hiking time should be 4-5 hours (about 7 miles). The climb to Belanger Pass (elevation 4350 feet) is gradual; as usual, expect wet feet as the trail zigzags across the small stream. The view of the Chugach during the descent from the pass is magnificent, a fitting climax to the trip (elevation loss about 1400 feet). Respect and circumvent private property encountered where the ORV trail joins Martin Road, two miles from the Glenn Highway. The trip ends at mile 123.3 on the Glenn Highway, at the junction of Martin Road and the Glenn Highway almost opposite Tahneta Inn. The road is marked by a sign for the Chickaloon-Knik-Nelchina Trail System. Park near the highway at Martin Road or ask permission to park cars at Tahneta Inn or at Gunsight Mountain Lodge, ¼ mile west.

CHICKALOON TO VALDEZ

50 Gunsight Mountain in Winter

Round trip 7 miles
Allow 8–10 hours
High point 6441 feet
Total elevation gain 3140 feet
Best February–April
USGS map Anchorage D2

Gunsight Mountain, about 70 miles west of Glennallen, is named for the distinct notch between its two summits. The trip is excellent for all, from the experienced mountaineer to the novice just trying winter climbing for the first time. The superb panorama, from the top, of the Wrangell, Chugach, and Talkeetna mountains, is well worth the effort. Proper winter gear, good physical condition, and, for the beginning winter mountaineer, experienced companions are necessary. Skiers will want climbing skins; snowshoes should be wrapped with heavy cord to provide greater traction on the steep slope. Lucky climbers may glimpse a band of caribou.

A summer climb of the peak requires some bushwhacking. The best approach in that season is via the Squaw Creek Trail (Trip 49), which climbs past the worst of the brush.

For a winter climb, drive northeast from Anchorage on the Glenn Highway to mile 118.4. Park in a pullout marked "Blueberry Hill trailhead" (elevation 3300 feet), near a side road from the south. The side road leads to the White Alice System radio relay site, visible in the distance.

Walk a short way west to a creek that crosses the Glenn Highway and don skis or snowshoes. Head northwest through light brush up the gully of the creek, gradually climbing the ridge above the left side of the stream. Head up the mountain, eventually veering southwest (left) toward the southeast summit (elevation 6441 feet), the higher but easier of the 2 summits. Most of the climb is gradual and poses no technical problems. For the last few hundred feet, which are much steeper, skis

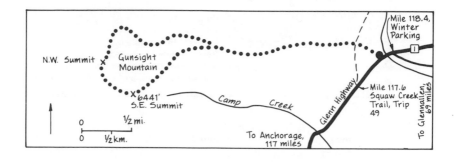

N.W. Summit ✕   Gunsight
                 Mountain

✕ 6441'
S.E. Summit   Camp   Creek

Mile 118.4,
Winter
Parking

Mile 117.6
Squaw Creek
Trail, Trip
49

Glenn Highway

To Glennallen,
69 miles

To Anchorage,
117 miles

0   ½ mi.
0   ½ km.

or snowshoes will have to be cached. Lug soles and perhaps crampons will be necessary for adequate traction to the summit.

A traverse of the notch and the ridge connecting the summits requires crampons and technical skill, especially in winter—it is not for beginners. Although not excessively difficult for experienced mountaineers, the route involves rappelling. To avoid the rappel, the notch can be bypassed on the back (south) side. An ascent of the northwest summit (elevation about 6440 feet) along the north ridge has some exposure but is also not technically difficult.

Winter temperatures frequently reach −25° to −40° F, and wind can increase the chill factor still further. Arctic winter clothing is absolutely necessary for a midwinter climb. Be sure to have adequate foot gear, preferably bunny boots or high-altitude, double climbing boots. Remember that Alaskan winter days are short; watch the time. Take a flashlight and keep its batteries warm inside your parka.

Gunsight Mountain from the Glenn Highway (Simmerman photo)

51 Gulkana River

Up to 80 miles
Allow 4–7 days
Gradient 16 feet/mile overall
Best late June–early September
USGS maps Gulkana B3, B4, C4, D4
Managed by Bureau of Land Management

Flowing through rolling, forested hill country with abundant wildlife and occasional views of the impressive Wrangell Mountains, the Gulkana River is ideal for a challenging and exciting kayak, raft, or canoe trip. Portions of the first part of the trip, from Paxson Lake to Sourdough Creek, are difficult; the rapids in this section should be run only in a raft or by experienced canoeists or kayakers. The second part of the trip, from Sourdough Creek to Gulkana, is suitable for canoeists with limited experience in rapids. Splash covers for canoes and kayaks are necessary for the Paxson–Sourdough section and recommended for the Sourdough–Gulkana section. If planning a trip on the first section in June, call Paxson Lodge to be sure the ice on Paxson Lake, which generally breaks up in mid-June, is gone.

Drive to mile 175, Richardson Highway (10.5 miles south of Paxson, 250 miles from Anchorage), and follow a 1.6-mile gravel road west to Paxson Lake Campground. Use the 500-foot boardwalk to portage across the marshy area between the campground and Paxson Lake. Paddle southwest along the shoreline to the lake's outlet and the start of the Gulkana River. An alternate access to the lake is at the boat ramp, located 4 miles north at the wayside at mile 179.5. The first part of the trip, from Paxson Lake Campground (1) to Sourdough Creek (6), is 45 miles long and takes about 4 days by raft, 3 days by canoe or kayak. River classifications used here are those designated by the International White Water Scale and defined more fully on page 20.

Paddle southwest on Paxson Lake to the outlet. The first 3 miles of the river consist of rocky, shallow rapids; the river drops 25 feet/mile in this stretch (WW3 canoeing, difficult). After the junction with Middle Fork (2) the river is pleasant and relatively calm for 15 miles (WW2, medium).

About 18 miles from Paxson Lake a canyon begins and with it about ¼ mile of rapids (3) (WW4, very difficult), the most difficult water described in this book. The river is deep but has rocks; the gradient is 50 feet/mile. Boaters will be able to see and hear the beginning of the rapids in plenty of time to get to shore. Boats can be portaged for this short distance along the left bank on a trail that begins just upstream of the first white water. Before deciding to run the rapids, all boaters

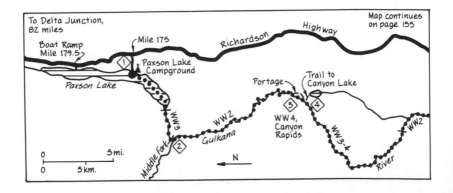

Gulkana River below Sourdough, August (Nienhueser photo)

should stop here and hike downstream for a good look. At the first bend after the portage, a 1-mile foot trail (4) leaving the left bank leads to Canyon Lake, a pleasant side trip.

The next 8 miles of the river are rough but not excessively difficult. The remainder of the river to Sourdough (6) is WW2. About 18 miles below Canyon Rapids the West Fork (5) of the Gulkana River enters from the right.

Campsites abound along the upper river. Leave a clean campsite, dispose of human waste properly, and use existing firepits or, better, a camping stove to reduce the impact on the forests. Boil all drinking water taken from the river itself.

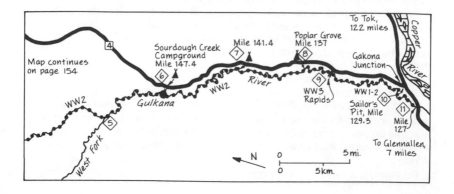

Map continues on page 154

155

Canyon Rapids, August (John Ireton photo)

From Paxson Lake to Sourdough the river is designated as a National Wild River.

Caution is the word for those traveling the upper section of the river. The entire 45 miles is far from the road system. The frigid Alaskan waters make capsizing particularly dangerous. Life jackets and wet suits or warm clothing should be worn and at least two boats should make the trip, always maintaining sufficient distance between them to allow complete freedom of route.

From Sourdough (6) to the Gulkana exit (11), 35 miles, the river closely parallels the highway. This section generally takes 1–2 days. Actual time on the river runs from 6–9 hours for canoes and kayaks and 8–12 hours for rafts. The shorter times apply when the river is high and fast. The gradient varies from 15–25 feet/mile and the major part of this section, with pleasant pools and interesting WW2 riffles, is not difficult. A short stretch, 50 yards, of WW3 rapids (9) is lots of fun.

The Sourdough entrance or exit (6) is at mile 147.4, Richardson Highway. The final take-out (11) is at mile 127, Richardson Highway, where the highway crosses the river. All access to the river here is over land owned by the Gulkana Village Corporation. The Corporation operates a campground and boat ramp (fees for use) on the east bank. Whether the highway right of way is public or private land will be decided in court.

Beginning just south of Sourdough Creek Campground the river passes through

Alaska Native land owned by the Ahtna Regional Corporation. Within these lands, those fishing from shore or camping must have an access permit (fee), available from the Ahtna Regional Corporation in Copper Center (address in the Appendix), the Ahtna Lodge in Glennallen, or Ahtna's river monitor on the river during fishing season. The question of who owns the river bottom, the state or Ahtna Regional Corporation, will be decided in the courts. If the state wins, the river's gravel bars will also be public land.

Between Sourdough and Gulkana, boaters may camp at three public 1-acre sites, marked by signs on the river. The first (7) is near mile 141.4, Richardson Highway; the second, Poplar Grove (8), is near mile 137; and the third, Sailor's Pit (10), is near mile 129.3. The campsites are connected to the Richardson Highway by ¼-mile-long foot trails. The trail from the highway to Poplar Grove begins in the southwest corner of a gravel pit near mile 137. Those taking a 1-day trip or wishing to avoid the WW3 rapids (9) can exit at Poplar Grove.

Along both sections of the river watch for moose, beaver, muskrat, otter, caribou, bear, bald eagles, and red foxes. Anglers are likely to catch lake trout, grayling, white fish, and burbot in Paxson Lake and king salmon, red salmon, rainbow trout, grayling, and white fish in the river.

CHICKALOON TO VALDEZ

52 Chitina Railroad Bed

Round trip 10 miles
Hiking time 5–8 hours
High point 550 feet
Total elevation gain 100 feet
Best May–October
USGS map Valdez B2

Take a walk into history on an easy scenic trail through Wood Canyon of the Copper River. The trail follows the bed of the railroad, which once carried ore from the copper-rich Kennicott-McCarthy area (Trip 53) to the seaport of Cordova. Watch for Indian graves, some with spirit houses, but do not disturb. An excellent hike for children and less agile outdoor buffs, the trail is mostly level, with a few dips to cross small creeks.

In 1899 a deposit of bornite ore, containing up to 85% copper, was discovered 60 miles east of Chitina. As staging area and the access to roads to Interior Alaska, Chitina became a busy community. (*Chiti* is an Indian word meaning copper; *na* means river.) The ore discovery brought intrigue, gun fights, and awesome riches. It

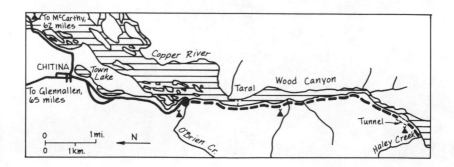

also brought a railroad. The Copper River and Northwestern Railroad, completed in 1911 at a cost of $23 million, was built to haul the ore to tidewater for shipment south. Then, in 1938, the mines shut down. The railroad was abandoned, and Chitina became a near ghost town. Later the iron rails were removed. In the 1950s, construction of a highway on the railroad grade began at the Cordova end. The 1964 earthquake collapsed one span of the railroad's famous Million Dollar Bridge (built in 1910) and the highway project was abandoned. Before hiking, you may want to read the engrossing story of the construction of the railroad, immortalized in Rex Beach's thinly disguised novel, *The Iron Trail*. For photos and additional history, see *The Copper Spike* by Lone E. Janson.

To reach the trailhead, drive to mile 82.6, Richardson Highway, turn east onto the Edgerton Highway, and continue 33 miles to Chitina (254 miles from Anchorage). Follow the highway left as it becomes Chitina's main street. Immediately on the right, two dirt roads go south from the main street. Take the left one, a shortcut to O'Brien Creek Road, turn right and, ignoring side roads, drive 3 miles to a public campground at O'Brien Creek (elevation 450 feet). The road, on the old railroad bed, is a single lane with a few short, very steep, winding hills unsuitable for large camper vehicles and trailers.

On foot, cross the O'Brien Creek bridge and follow the trail south along the impressive Copper River and through a tunnel. Upriver, Mt. Wrangell looms in the distance; downstream the Copper River bends around the cliffs of Wood Canyon. A fine destination for a family overnight is Haley Creek, with a sandy beach campsite and a roaring waterfall. The historic trail continues south of Haley Creek but is overgrown and very hard to find.

Old trestle in Wood Canyon, July (Simmerman photo)

The trail passes numerous other good picnic and campsites en route. Water is available at O'Brien Creek, at the second stream beyond it, and at Haley Creek. Other streams flow intermittently. During the June and July salmon runs, the banks of the Copper River are lined with dip netters; parking and camping spots may be hard to find, and the trail is noisy with off-road vehicles. For roadside camping, follow Chitina's main street through town and across the Copper River bridge; a campground is on the right.

CHICKALOON TO VALDEZ

53 KENNECOTT MINES

Round trip 8 miles plus 10 road miles
Hiking time 1 or 2 days
High point 6050 feet
Total elevation gain 4700 feet
Best June–September
USGS maps McCarthy B5, B6, C5
Wrangell–St. Elias National Park

Early 1900 buildings of the Kennecott Copper Corporation company town and the nearby once-boistrous town of McCarthy sit decaying and silent beside the Kennicott Glacier. High above, on precipitous mountain slopes, mines once disgorged precious blue-green ore onto aerial trams for transporting to the mill 4500 feet below. Abandoned roads leading up to two of the mines, Bonanza and Jumbo, are trails into history.

The Kennicott copper deposit, which became the Bonanza Mine, was reportedly found in 1900 by two prospectors looking for a horse pasture. They mistook the distant outcropping of malachite (copper carbonate) for green grass. Nearby Jumbo Mine tapped the largest deposit in the area, producing 70,000 tons of 70% copper (with 20 ounces of silver per ton). The entire production of the Kennecott mines

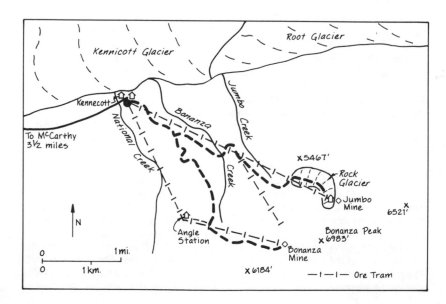

Jumbo Mine buildings, August (Simmerman photo)

assayed an average of 13% copper. A honeycomb of more than 70 miles of layered tunnels connects the Erie, Jumbo, Bonanza and Mother Lode mines. When the rich veins played out and the mines closed in 1938, the towns died. Through the years, Alaskans who prefer a quiet, remote lifestyle have been reclaiming the settlements.

Drive to mile 82.6, Richardson Highway, turn east onto the Edgerton Highway, and continue 33 miles to Chitina (254 miles from Anchorage). Expect no gas or groceries beyond here. Follow the main road through Chitina and cross Copper River on a massive bridge. The 63-mile, single-lane, primitive gravel road ahead of you follows the bed of the old Copper River and Northwestern Railroad, which carried ore from Kennecott to Cordova from 1911 to 1938 (see Trip 52). The road is not recommended for large camper vehicles or trailers. Allow 4 hours to drive the rough road and expect flats; railroad spikes redistributed by road graders threaten tires. The road terminates at the Kennicott River. Park in the upper area. A glacier-dammed lake breaks out each summer, flooding low areas near the river for a day.

To reach McCarthy and Kennecott, two channels of the turbulent Kennicott River must be crossed. Local residents have erected hand-operated cable trams capable of transporting 2 people and their packs. Lightweight bicycles can be tied onto clips on the side. Residents assume no liability for the safety of the tram system.

After crossing the Kennicott River, follow the gravel road east, up a small rise to an intersection and the McCarthy museum, an old red railroad depot well worth a visit. The left fork of the road goes to Kennecott, 5 miles away. The right fork leads into Mc-Carthy. (An alternate access to McCarthy is to fly to the air strip, just outside of town.

Planes can be chartered in the Glennallen-Gulkana area or take the Tuesday mail plane, making arrangements through Ellis Air Service (address in the Appendix).

Be sure to visit the McCarthy Lodge, built in the early 1900s and full of relics and old photographs; meals, drinks and showers are available. Ask about the two spellings of Kennecott. Campers are asked to tent near the Kennicott River. Clear Creek, which you will cross as you walk to the townsite, supplies drinking water to the residents; be careful not to contaminate it. Please remember that ALL structures and land in McCarthy and Kennecott are privately owned—do not enter buildings, take relics, or use old lumber for firewood.

To reach the mines, walk or bicycle the road north from the museum to Kennecott or contact the McCarthy Lodge for a ride (charge). In Kennecott, cross the bridge over National Creek (fill your canteen here) and turn right up a gravel road that parallels the creek. The road skirts the top of the mill, before climbing steeply toward the mines.

After about an hour of steady but leisurely climbing, as the road bears right, an obscure, mostly overgrown trail goes left through the alders. The trail, which may be marked by flagging, leads to Jumbo Mine, high in a cirque at 5800 feet elevation. The main road continues to the tram angle station and Bonanza Mine.

The Jumbo Mine trail, an old road and quite walkable, crosses Bonanza Creek (good campsite) in less than a mile. Brush is left behind at 3700 feet, and by 4700 feet the trail winds up a massive rock glacier. Water and a campsite are at the lower end of the glacier. Since the slope faces south, the climb can be very hot on a sunny day. Follow the old road all the way up the rock glacier as it bears right into the cirque below Bonanza Peak (elevation 6983 feet).

To reach Bonanza Mine (elevation 5950 feet), instead of taking the Jumbo Mine trail, continue up the main road. At an intersection near the tram, take the left fork; the right-hand trail leads to a privately owned cabin at the angle station. No buildings remain at the Bonanza Mine, but the scenery is well worth the climb.

CHICKALOON TO VALDEZ

54 Worthington Glacier Overlook

Round trip 2 miles
Hiking time 2-3 hours
High point 3400 feet
Total elevation gain 1200 feet
Best late June–September
USGS map Valdez A5

Enter the lofty mountain realm of sculptured blue glacier ice. Climb an easy trail to look deep into crevasses, all the while standing on firm ground near soft green meadows. This charming alpine trail near Thompson Pass barely leaves the roadside. It is a refreshing leg-stretcher that gives a hint of the thrill of mountaineering.

Don't let cloudy or misty weather cancel the hike. The blue of the ice is more intense on gray days, and the mountains are more mysterious. The first part of the trail offers easy, secure hiking; the last part is exposed, with a precipitous drop to the glacier far below.

From mile 29.4, Richardson Highway (273 miles from Anchorage), follow a side road west to the Worthington Glacier State Recreation Site. Park in the lower area with the picnic shelter (elevation 2200 feet). To the left of the glacier, near the icefalls, stands a prominent gray knob, a good destination if you are a skilled hiker. Those less skilled will enjoy climbing to the meadow.

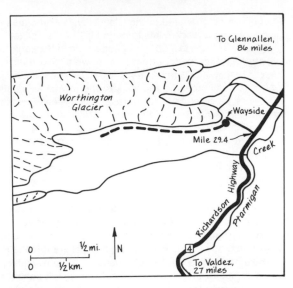

To find the trail from the parking area, walk west up the moraine and climb to its crest. Worn by use, the trail is easy to follow, winding through small willow patches and up a lush green meadow of heather, mosses, and wildflowers. On a sunny day, the meadow is a fine spot for a picnic. If children are along, watch that they don't approach the cliffs above the glacier.

The more adventurous can continue to parallel the glacier edge, climbing the moraine as far as is comfortable. The trail is frequently exposed, requiring sure footing and boots with good traction. On rainy days in particular the moraine can be slippery; a fall could be serious, perhaps fatal. However, with caution, this little hike is one of the most delightful in Southcentral Alaska.

Worthington Glacier Trail, August (Simmerman photo)

The route has no drinking water. Camp at the Blueberry Lake State Recreation Site, mile 24, Richardson Highway.

The whole Thompson Pass area offers good easy hiking above timberline on heather and smooth bedrock. The area is exceptionally scenic when autumn frosts turn the tundra a brilliant red.

CHICKALOON TO VALDEZ

55 Mineral Creek Valley

Round trip 2 miles
Hiking time 1–2 hours
High point 650 feet
Total elevation gain 100 feet
Best June–September
USGS map Valdez A7

For the visitor to Valdez who is looking for a breath of fresh air and a stretch, a walk along Mineral Creek is the answer. The trail is an old roadbed through a narrow, lush green canyon. Beautiful on a sunny day, it is even more dramatic when low clouds swirl through the canyon, changing moods from moment to moment. Someday this may be a route to the tempting alpine country surrounding Valdez, but at present the trail ends in brush; further travel is difficult and unpleasant.

Valdez can be reached either from the Richardson Highway or via the Alaska State passenger and auto ferry from Whittier or Cordova. Ferry foot passengers must walk 6½ road miles to reach the trailhead.

Entering downtown Valdez, the Richardson Highway becomes Egan Drive. Turn

Smith Mill, July (Simmerman photo)

Alaska state ferry M.V. Bartlett *at Whittier (Simmerman photo)*

right (north) off Egan Drive onto Hazelet Avenue, go 10 blocks to Hanagita Drive, and turn left. Drive 1 block and turn right onto Mineral Creek Road. At the top of the rise continue straight ahead, not up to the water tanks. Drive this scenic, but poorly maintained, gravel road 5.5 miles and park (elevation 550 feet).

On foot, continue on the old roadbed, paralleling Mineral Creek but keeping well above the rushing water. On the right, just before Brevier Creek, is the historic Smith Mill. This ore-crushing mill once processed gold-bearing rock from the numerous mines in the area.

Sometimes, local efforts keep the trail cleared a distance beyond Brevier Creek, but most visitors will want to stop here. To reach high country requires considerable bushwhacking. The entire Valdez area is extremely brushy except on recently glaciated slopes, where shrubs have not yet had time to grow. Additional hiking trails are needed to appreciate fully this immensely scenic area.

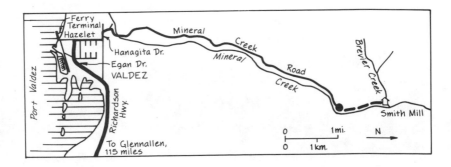

September morning in Interior Alaska (Simmerman photo)

Canada geese and young (Simmerman photo)

APPENDIX

———— TIME OF YEAR ————

Summer trips are listed under the first month the routes are generally free enough of snow for use. Conditions vary greatly from year to year.

APRIL
1 Homer Beach Walk
10 Race Point
26 Bird Ridge
28 Table Rock
29 Old Johnson Trail

MAY
2 Swan Lake and Swanson River Canoe Routes (late May)
3 Seven Lakes Trail
4 Hidden Creek Trail
4 Kenai River Trail
5 Skilak Lake Lookout
7 Kenai River
8 Russian Lakes
12 Ptarmigan Lake
14 Caribou Creek (cabin)
14 Trout, Juneau and Swan Lakes (cabins)
16 Hope Point
17 Gull Rock
19 Byron Glacier View
23 Winner Creek Gorge (late May)
27 Indian Valley
28 Table Rock and beyond
36 Rendezvous Peak
38 The Perch
40 Thunder Bird Falls
43 Lazy Mountain
52 Chitina Railroad Bed

JUNE
6 Fuller Lakes
6 Skyline Trail
8 Russian Lakes/Cooper Lake Trail
8 Resurrection River Trail
9 Crescent Lake/Carter Lake
11 Lost Lake (late June)
13 Johnson Pass
14 Resurrection Pass Trail System
23 Winner Creek Trail
25 Crow Pass (mid-June)
25 Crow Pass to Eagle River (mid-June)
27 Indian Pass
30 Rabbit Lake
31 Flattop
32 The Ramp
33 Williwaw Lakes
34 Wolverine Peak
35 Knoya and Tikishla Peaks
35 North Fork Campbell Creek
37 Eagle Lake
37 Eagle River Overlook
39 Round Top and Black Tail Rocks
41 Twin Peaks Trail, to brushline
42 Bold Peak Valley
48 Hicks Creek/Chitna Pass
49 Syncline Mountain
51 Gulkana River
53 Kennecott Mines
54 Worthington Glacier Overlook (late June)
55 Mineral Creek Valley

JULY
15 Palmer Creek Lakes
18 Turnagain Pass
21 Portage Pass
22 Alyeska Glacier View
22 Mt. Alyeska "Summit"
41 East Twin Pass
43 Matanuska Peak
44 Reed Lakes
46 Craigie Creek
47 Peters Hills
50 Gunsight Mountain in summer

WINTER

1 Homer Beach Walk
2 Swan Lake and Swanson River Canoe Trails (ski touring)
3 Seven Lakes Trail
4 Hidden Creek Trail
4 Kenai River Trail
5 Skilak Lake Lookout
8 Russian Lakes/Resurrection River Trail System
9 Carter Lake
11 Lost Lake
13 Johnson Pass Trailhead areas
14 Resurrection Pass Trail, Hope to Sterling Highway
18 Turnagain Pass Ski Tour
18 Tincan Ridge
20 Bear Valley Ski Tour
23 Winner Creek Gorge
23 Alyeska Cross-Country Ski Trails
24 Glacier Creek Ski Tour
26 Bird Ridge (hiking)
27 Indian Valley
27 Ship Creek to Indian
29 Old Johnson Trail (skiing or hiking)
31 Flattop
32 The Ramp, to the pass
33 Williwaw Lakes
33 Middle Fork Loop Ski System
34 Wolverine Road
34 Wolverine Peak
36 Rendezvous Peak
37 Eagle Lake
38 The Perch
39 Round Top and Black Tail Rocks
44 Reed Lakes
45 Hatcher Pass Ski Tour
45 Independence Mine Bowl
48 Hicks Creek/Chitna Pass
49 Syncline Mountain
50 Gunsight Mountain

———— LENGTH OF TRIP ————

Driving time is not considered in listing trip length.

SHORT (half-day or less)

1 Homer Beach Walk
3 Seven Lakes Trail, part of
4 Hidden Creek Trail
5 Skilak Lake Lookout
6 Lower Fuller Lake
8 Lower Russian Lake
9 Carter Lake
9 Crescent Creek, lower bridge
10 Race Point
12 Ptarmigan Lake, west end
13 Bench Creek bridge
14 Juneau Falls
15 Palmer Creek Lakes
16 Hope Point, first mile
18 Turnagain Pass Ski Tour
18 Turnagain Pass in summer
19 Byron Glacier View
20 Bear Valley Ski Tour

21 Portage Pass
22 Alyeska Glacier View (chairlift up and down)
22 Alyeska Glacier View (walk down)
23 Alyeska Cross-Country Ski Trails
24 Glacier Creek Ski Tour
25 Monarch Mine
25 Crow Pass
26 Bird Ridge
28 Table Rock
29 Old Johnson Trail
31 Flattop
34 Wolverine Peak, to brushline (summer)
34 Wolverine Road (winter)
36 Rendezvous Peak
38 The Perch
39 Black Tail Rocks
40 Thunder Bird Falls
41 Twin Peaks Trail, to brushline
45 Hatcher Pass Ski Tour, part of
45 Independence Mine Bowl (winter or summer)
47 Peters Hills
52 Chitina Railroad Bed
53 McCarthy and Kennecott
54 Worthington Glacier Overlook
55 Mineral Creek Valley

DAY TRIPS

1 Homer Beach Walk
3 Seven Lakes Trail
4 Kenai River Trail/Hidden Creek Trail
6 Fuller Lakes
7 Kenai River, part of
8 Lower Russian Lake and Cascades
9 Crescent Lake via Crescent Creek
9 Crescent Lake via Carter Lake
11 Lost Lake
11 Lost Lake to Primrose Campground
12 Ptarmigan Lake, east end
14 Caribou Creek (cabin)
14 Trout Lake (cabin)
15 Palmer Creek Lakes
16 Hope Point
17 Gull Rock
18 Turnagain Pass Ski Tour
18 Tincan Ridge Ski Touring
21 Portage Pass
22 Mt. Alyeska, "summit" from chairlift
22 Alyeska Glacier View, from bottom
23 Winner Creek Gorge
24 Glacier Creek Ski Tour
25 Crow Pass
26 Bird Ridge
27 Indian Valley
28 Table Rock and beyond
29 Old Johnson Trail
30 Rabbit Lake
31 Flattop and beyond
32 The Ramp
32 Powerline Pass
32 The Wedge
33 Williwaw Lakes
34 Wolverine Peak
35 Knoya Peak

35 North Fork Campbell Creek
36 Rendezvous Peak and beyond
37 Eagle Lake
37 Eagle River Overlook
38 The Iditarod Trail
39 Black Tail Rocks
39 Round Top
39 Vista Peak
41 East Twin Pass
42 Bold Peak Valley
43 Lazy Mountain
44 Reed Lakes
45 Hatcher Pass Ski Tour
46 Craigie Creek and beyond
47 Peters Hills
48 Hicks Creek/Pinochle Creek Trail
49 Belanger Pass
50 Gunsight Mountain (winter or summer)
52 Chitina Railroad Bed
53 Kennecott Mines

STRENUOUS DAY TRIPS
6 Skyline Trail Traverse
8 Cooper Lake to Russian Lakes
8 Upper Russian Lake
13 Johnson Pass
14 Resurrection Pass via Summit Creek and
   Devil's Pass Trails
14 Juneau and Swan Lakes
18 Tincan Ridge Ski Touring
22 Alyeska "Summit" from bottom
23 Winner Creek Trail
26 Bird Ridge
28 McHugh Peak via Table Rock
28 McHugh Peak via Rabbit Lake
30 Tikishla Peak
37 Eagle Lake and beyond
38 The Iditarod Trail
42 Bold Peak Valley
43 Matanuska Peak
46 Craigie Creek and beyond
47 Peters Hills

DAY TRIPS THAT
MAKE OVERNIGHTS
3 Seven Lakes Trail
4 Hidden Creek Trail
4 Kenai River Trail
6 Fuller Lakes
8 Lower Russian Lake
9 Crescent Lake (cabin)
9 Carter Lake
11 Lost Lake
11 Lost Lake to Primrose Campground
12 Ptarmigan Lake, either end
14 Caribou Creek (cabin)
14 Trout Lake (cabin)
15 Palmer Creek Lakes
21 Portage Pass
24 Glacier Creek Ski Tour
25 Crow Pass (cabin)
27 Indian Pass
30 Rabbit Lake
32 The Ramp
33 Williwaw Lakes
35 Knoya Peak

35 North Fork Campbell Creek
37 Eagle Lake
38 The Perch
38 The Iditarod Trail
42 Bold Peak Valley
44 Reed Lakes
46 Craigie Creek area
47 Peters Hills
49 Belanger Pass
50 Gunsight Mountain (winter or summer)
52 Chitina Railroad Bed
53 Kennecott Mines

OVERNIGHT TRIPS
2 Swan Lake and Swanson River Canoe
   Routes
6 Skyline Trail Traverse
7 Kenai River, part of
8 Upper Russian Lake (cabins)
8 Cooper Lake to Russian Lakes (cabins)
8 Russian Lakes to Resurrection River
   (cabins)
8 Cooper Lake to Resurrection River
11, 8 Lost Lake (11) to Cooper Lake (8)
13 Johnson Pass
14 Devil's Pass/Resurrection Pass Trails to
   the Sterling Highway (cabin)
14 Resurrection Pass via Summit Creek and
   Devil's Pass Trails (cabin)
14 East Creek (cabin)
14 Juneau and Swan Lakes (cabins)
23 Winner Creek Trail
27 Ship Creek to Indian
30 Suicide Peaks
32, 27 The Ramp (32) to Indian (27)
33, 35 Williwaw Lakes to North Fork Campbell Creek
35 Tikishla Peak
46 Craigie Creek and beyond
47 Peters Hills
48 Hicks Creek/Pinochle Creek Trail
48 Purinton Creek Trail
51 Gulkana River, lower section
53 Kennecott Mines

TRIPS OF THREE DAYS OR MORE
2 Swan Lake and Swanson River Canoe
   Routes
7 Kenai River
8 Russian Lakes/Resurrection River Trails
14, 8 Resurrection Pass (14)/Russian Lakes/
   Resurrection River Trails (8)
25 Crow Pass to Eagle River
46 Craigie Creek and beyond
48 Hicks Creek/Chitna Pass
49 Syncline Mountain
51 Gulkana River

———— CANOE, RAFT ————
OR KAYAK TRIPS
2 Swan Lake and Swanson River Canoe
   Routes
7 Kenai River
51 Gulkana River

Tarn above Palmer Creek, August—Trip 15 (Simmerman photo)

—GOOD TRIPS FOR CHILDREN—

1 Homer Beach Walk
2 Swan Lake and Swanson River Canoe Routes
3 Seven Lakes Trail
4 Hidden Creek Trail
5 Skilak Lake Lookout
6 Fuller Lakes
8 Lower Russian Lake
9 Crescent Lake (overnight, cabin)
9 Crescent Lake via Carter Lake
11 Lost Lake (overnight)
12 Ptarmigan Lake, west end (overnight)
13 Bench Creek bridge
14 Juneau Falls
14 Resurrection Pass Trail System (5-day trip, cabins)
14 Caribou Creek (overnight, cabin)
14 Trout Lake (overnight, cabin)
15 Palmer Creek Lakes
16 Hope Point, first mile*
17 Gull Rock
18 Turnagain Pass in summer
18 Turnagain Pass Ski Tour
18 Tincan Ridge Ski Touring
19 Byron Glacier View
20 Bear Valley Ski Tour
21 Portage Pass
22 Alyeska Glacier View via chairlift
23 Winner Creek Gorge*
23 Alyeska Cross-Country Ski Trails
24 Glacier Creek Ski Tour

25 Monarch Mine
25 Crow Pass (overnight, cabin)
26 Bird Ridge*
27 Indian Valley
28 Table Rock
29 Old Johnson Trail
30 Rabbit Lake
31 Flattop*
32 The Ramp, to the pass
32 The Wedge
34 Wolverine Road
34 Middle Fork Loop Ski System
36 Rendezvous Peak
38 The Perch
39 Round Top and Black Tail Rocks
40 Thunder Bird Falls
41 Twin Peaks Trail, to brushline
42 Bold Peak Valley*
43 Lazy Mountain*
45 Independence Mine Bowl (summer or winter)
46 Craigie Creek
47 Peters Hills
52 Chitina Railroad Bed
53 McCarthy and Kennecott
54 Worthington Glacier Overlook, first ½ mile
55 Mineral Creek Valley

*These trips are more difficult, but are recommended for experienced children.

─── TRIPS ACCESSIBLE FROM PUBLIC TRANSPORTATION ───

The following trips may be reached by bus, train, ferry, or scheduled air service, though daily or year-round service may not be available. If an additional short distance by road must be traveled on foot, a trip is included; additional miles one way are noted.

Numbers key each trip to public transportation as follows:

(1) Intercity bus lines, with main offices in Anchorage, serve Southcentral Alaska.
(2) Anchorage Public Transit, "The People Mover," 632 Sixth Avenue, Pouch 6-650, Anchorage, AK 99502, phone (907) 264-6543.
(3) Alaska Marine Highway (state ferry), 213 West 6th Avenue, Anchorage, AK 99501, phone (907) 272-4482. Toll free numbers: (in Alaska) (800) 551-7185; (Outside) (800) 544-2251.
(4) Alaska Railroad, Pouch 7-2111, Anchorage, AK 99510, phone (907) 265-2494 (schedules); (907) 265-2623 (reservations).
(5) Scheduled air service. See your travel agent.

1 Homer Beach Walk (5) + 1 mile
3 Seven Lakes Trail (1)
4 Kenai River Trail (1)
6 Fuller Lakes (1)
6 Skyline Trail (1)
7 Kenai River (collapsible boat) (1)
8 Russian Lakes (1) + 1 mile
8 Resurrection River Trail (1) + 7.5 miles
9 Crescent Lake (1) + 3.3 miles
9 Carter Lake (1)
10 Race Point (1)
11 Lost Lake (1)
11 Primrose Trail (1) + 1 mile
12 Ptarmigan Lake, both trailheads (1)
13 Johnson Pass, both trailheads (1)
14 Resurrection Pass, Sterling Highway trailhead (1)
14 Devil's Pass Trail (1)
14 Summit Creek Trail (1)
18 Turnagain Pass Ski Tour (1)
21 Portage Pass (3) or (4)
22 Alyeska Glacier View (1) or (3), + 3 miles
23 Winner Creek Gorge (1) or (3), + 3 miles, (1) + 3 miles in winter
24 Glacier Creek Ski Tour (1) + 2 miles

25 Crow Pass (1) or (3), + 7.5 miles
26 Bird Ridge (1)
27 Indian Valley (1) + 1.3 miles
28 Table Rock (1)
29 Old Johnson Trail (1)
30 Rabbit Lake (2) + 2.2 miles
31 Flattop (2) + 2.6 miles
32 The Ramp (2) + 2.6 miles
32 Powerline Pass Traverse, (1) and (2), + 3.9 miles
33 Williwaw Lakes (2) + 2.6 miles
34 Wolverine Peak (2) + 2 miles
35 Knoya and Tikishla Peaks (2) + 2 miles
39 Round Top and Black Tail Rocks, (1) or (2), + 1 mile
40 Thunder Bird Falls (1)
43 Lazy Mountain (1) + 4 miles
48 Hicks Creek/Chitna Pass, both trailheads (1)
49 Syncline Mountain, both trailheads (1)
50 Gunsight Mountain (1)
51 Gulkana River (collapsible boat) (1)
53 Kennecott Mines (5)

INFORMATION SOURCES

Land Managers:
Chugach National Forest, 201 East Ninth Avenue, Anchorage, AK (99501), phone (907) 279-5541. Cabin reservations: above address, phone (907) 276-0472, or through any U.S. Forest Service office in the state. Recreation information recording, (907) 274-4113. **Avalanche and mountain weather forecast recording:** (907) 271-4500 (Anchorage). Chugach National Forest has branch offices at Cordova [P.O. Box 280 (99574), phone (907) 424-7661] and Seward [P.O.Box 275 (99664), phone (907) 224-3374].

Chugach State Park, Alaska Division of Parks, 2601 Commercial Drive, Anchorage, AK 99501, phone (907) 279-3413. Recreation information recording, (907) 274-6713. **Avalanche and mountain weather forecast recording,** (907) 271-4500.

Gulkana National Wild River, Bureau of Land Management, P.O. Box 147, Glennallen, AK 99588, phone (907) 267-1369 (Anchorage), (907) 822-3217 (Glennallen).

Kenai National Wildlife Refuge, P.O. Box 2139, Soldotna, AK 99669, phone (907) 262-7021.

Kenai River Manager, Alaska Division of Parks and Outdoor Recreation, P.O. Box 1247, Soldotna, AK 99669, phone (907) 262-5581.

Additional Information Sources:
Ahtna Regional Corporation, Ahtna, Inc., Drawer G, Copper Center, AK 99753, phone (907) 822-3476.

Alaska Avalanche School, Alaska Division of Parks and Outdoor Recreation, Pouch 7-005, Anchorage, AK 99510, phone (907) 276-2653.

Alaska Division of Tourism, Pouch E-28, Juneau, AK 99811, phone (907) 465-2010. Ask for the "Vacation Planner," a publication, revised annually, which lists names, addresses and phone numbers of businesses and services of interest to the traveler, e.g. car rentals and guide services, including those offering canoe and raft trips.

Alaska Wilderness Guides Association, P.O. Box 98061, Anchorage, AK 99508, phone (907) 276-6634.

Alaska Railroad. See "Trips Accessible From Public Transportation" section.

Alyeska Mountain Nugget Inn, Alyeska Resort, P.O. Box 249, Girdwood, AK 99587, phone (907) 783-2222.

Canoe Rentals:
    Anchorage
    The Rental Room, 5905 Lake Otis Parkway (99507), phone (907) 562-2866.

    Soldotna
    Alaska Pioneer Canoers Assn., Box 931, (99669), phone (907) 262-4003; Roland's Sports Den, Box 2861, (99669), phone (907) 262-7491; Ron's Rent-It Center, Box 3370, (99669), phone (907) 262-5235.

    Sterling
    Pedersen's Moose River Resort, Mile 82, Star Route, (99672), phone (907) 262-4515.

Cooperative Extension Service, 2651 Providence Drive, Anchorage, AK 99508, phone (907) 786-1080.

Ellis Air Taxi, P.O. Box 105, Glennallen, AK 99588, phone (907) 822-3368.

Highway and Road Conditions: Alaska Department of Transportation, Maintenance and Operations Division, Pouch 6900, Anchorage, AK 99502, phone (907) 243-7675.

Parks and Forests Information Center, 605 West 4th Avenue, Anchorage, AK 99501. Opens in 1986. Until then, located at 2525 Gambell Street, Anchorage, AK 99503, phone (907) 271-4243 or 271-4245.

U.S. Geological Survey, Alaska topographic maps, over the counter sales: Public Inquiries Office, 4230 University Drive (Alaska Pacific University Campus), Anchorage, AK 99508-4664, phone (907) 561-5555. A limited stock of maps is available at the Federal Building, Earth Sciences Office, 701 C Street, Room 146, or P.O. Box 53, Anchorage, AK 99513, phone (907) 271-4308.

—— ORGANIZATIONS CONCERNED ABOUT ALASKA'S FUTURE ——

Alaskan Organizations:

Alaska Center for the Environment
1069 West Sixth Avenue
Anchorage, AK 99501
phone (907) 274-3621 or 279-8315

Alaskan Conservation Foundation
340 G Street, Room 201
Anchorage, AK 99501
phone (907) 276-1917

Friends of the Earth
1069 West Sixth Avenue
Anchorage, AK 99501
phone (907) 272-7335 or 272-1017

Mountaineering Club of Alaska
Box 2037
Anchorage, AK 99510

National Audubon Society
125 Christensen Drive
Anchorage, AK 99501
phone (907) 276-7034

Northern Alaska Environmental Center
218 Driveway
Fairbanks, AK 99701
phone (907) 452-5021

Sierra Club
241 East Fifth Avenue, Suite 205
Anchorage, AK 99501
phone (907) 276-4048

The Wilderness Society
519 West Eighth Avenue, Suite 205
Anchorage, AK 99501
phone (907) 272-9453

National Organizations:

Friends of the Earth
1045 Sansome Street
San Francisco, CA 94111

National Audubon Society
950 Third Avenue
New York, NY 10022

Sierra Club
530 Bush Street
San Francisco, CA 94108

Wilderness Society
1400 Eye Street, N.W.–Tenth Floor
Washington, D.C. 20006

INDEX

Boldfacing indicates major hikes. Italic page numbers refer to captions.

Ahtna Regional Corporation—157
Alder Creek—65
Alfred Creek—145, 149, 151, 152
Alyeska Creek—80, 81
Alyeska Glacier View—79-81
Alyeska, Mt.—79-81
Anchorage, north of—116-43
Anchorage Bowl—101-15
Anchorage watershed—103-15
Arctic Valley Ski Area—114
Ascension, Mt.—57
avalanches—24-27, *25, 26*

Bear Valley Ski Tour—75-77
bears—19-20
Belanger Pass—149, 151, 152
Bench Creek—61-62, 71
Bench Lake—61
Bird Ridge—89-91, *90*
Black Prospect Mine—140-41
Black Tail Rocks—122-24
boating—20-22, 47-50
Bold Peak—130, *130*
Bold Peak Valley—129-31
Boulder Creek—*146,* 148
Brevier Creek—164
Byron Creek—74
Byron Glacier—*75*
Byron Glacier View—74-75
Byron Peak—*75*

Calliope—118
Campbell Creek—106-107, 108-109,
    112-13, *112*
campfires—16
Cantata—118
Canyon Lake—155
Canyon Rapids—155, *156*
Caribou Creek—145, 147, *149*
Caribou Creek cabin—63
Carter Lake—53-54
Center Creek—61-62
Center Ridge—*70, 71,* 80
Chickaloon-Knik-Nelchina Trail—148, 152
Chickaloon to Valdez—144-65
children, hiking with—15
Chitina—157-59
Chitina Railroad Bed—157-59
Chitna Creek—147
Chitna Pass—145-48, *145*
Chugach Mountains—*31,* 122
Chugach National Forest—15, 89
Chugach State Park—14, 15, 118
Clear Creek—88, 161
clothing—22-23
Cooper Lake—52

Cooper Landing—47
Copper River—158-59
Craigie Creek—136, 139-41
Crescent Creek Trail—54
Crescent Lake—53-54, *53*
Crow Creek—85
Crow Pass—86-89, *87*
Crystal Lake—*87,* 88

Denali—141, *142*
Denali State Park—142
Devil's Pass—63, 64
Divide Lake—78
Dogsled Pass—139-41, *140*

Eagle Glacier—*88*
Eagle Lake—118-19
Eagle Peak—118
Eagle River—88-89, 118-19, *119, 120,* 121
Eagle River Overlook—118-19
Eagle River Visitors' Center—89, 121
East Creek cabin—63
East Twin Pass—127-29
Eklutna Lake—127-28, *128,* 129, *130,* 131
Engineer Lake—*29,* 40, *40*
equipment—15-16, 23

Flattop—103-105, *104*
Forks Roadhouse—141
frostbite—24
Fuller Lakes—44-46, *45*

Gavia Lake—*36,* 37, 38
Gene Lake—38
giardia—16-17
Glacier Creek—*22, 84, 85,* 134
Glacier Creek Ski Tour—83-86
Glacier Lake—*88*
Granite Creek—60
Gulkana River—21, 154-57, *155*
Gulkana Village Corporation—156
Gull Rock—68-69, *68*
Gunsight Creek—149
Gunsight Mountain—149, 152-53, *153*

Haley Creek, 158
Hatcher Pass—*30,* 133, *137*
Hatcher Pass Ski Tour—135-38
Hicks Creek—145-48
Hicks Creek Trail—146
Hicks Lake—147
Hidden Creek Trail—41-42
Hidden Lake—40, 106
Hikers Lake—39
Hikers' Trail—55-56, *55*
Homer—34

Homer Beach Walk—34-35, *35*
Hope—63, 64
Hope Point—66-67
Hunter Creek Pass—130
hypothermia—18-19

Icicle Creek—89
Iditarod Trail—81, 86, 91, 121
Independence Mine State Historic
   Park—136, 138, *138*
Indian—91-92, 106
Indian Creek Pass—91, *92*
Indian Pass Trail—86
Indian Valley—91-93, 106

Johnson Creek—61, 69
Johnson Lake—*61*
Johnson Pass—60-62
Juneau Creek—63
Juneau Creek Falls—63
Juneau Lake cabin—63

Kachemak Bay—34
Kelly Lake—39, 40
Kenai—47
Kenai Lake—47, 57-58
Kenai National Wildlife Refuge—15
Kenai Peninsula—14, 33-71, *104*
Kenai River—46-50, *48, 49*
Kenai River Trail—*32,* **42**
Kennecott—160-61
Kennecott Mines—159-61
Kennicott Glacier—159
Kennicott River—160
Knoya Peak—111-13

Lazy Mountain—131-33, *132*
Little Peters Creek—122-23
Long Point—141, 142
Lost Lake—*8, 31,* **56-58,** *57*
Lyon Creek—70
Lynx Peak—135

Marathon Mountain—55, 56
Matanuska Peak—131-33
Matanuska Valley Moose Range—147
"Max's Mountain"—81
McCarthy—159, 160-61
McHugh Creek—94, *96,* 97, 98, 103
McKinley, Mt.—*142*
Meadow Creek—123-24
Mineral Creek Valley—163-64
Monarch Mine—87
Monarch Peak—*143,* 147
moose—19
Moose River—37-38, 48
Mud Bay—35

Near Point—112-13

O'Brien Creek—158-59
Old Johnson Trail—94, **95-98,** *97*

Palmer Creek—64-65, *65*
Palmer Creek Lakes—64-65
Pass Creek—152
Passage Canal—78
Paxson Lake—20, 154-57
Perch, The—121-22
Peters Creek—141
Peters Hills—141-43, *142*
Petersville—142
Pinochle Creek Trail—146
Placer Creek—76, *76*
Poplar Grove—157
Porcupine Creek—58, 66
Portage Glacier—75-77, 78, *79*
Portage Lake—*72, 74,* 75-77, 78, *79*
Portage Pass—*14,* **77-79**
Portage to Potter—73-99
Potter—97-98
Powerline Pass—106, 107
Powerline Pass Trail—93
Primrose Trail—57-58
Ptarmigan Creek—58-60
Ptarmigan Lake—58-60, *59*
Ptarmigan Peak—102
Purinton Creek Trail—148
Puritan Creek trail—148

Rabbit Lake—102-103, *103*
Race Point—55-56
Rainbow Creek—97
Rainbow Valley—97, 98
Ramp, The—105-107, *107*
Raven Creek—88, 134
Raven Glacier—88
Reed Lakes—133-35, *134*
Rendezvous Peak—113-15, *115*
Resurrection Creek—63
Resurrection Pass Trail—62-64
Resurrection River Trail—50-52, *51*
Resurrection River valley—66
river classification—21
Round Top—122-24
Runners' Trail—56
Russian Lakes—50-52
Russian River—50

Sailors' Pit—157
Schooner Bend—47
Seven Lakes Trail—39-40
Seward—55, *55*
Ship Creek—92-93, 106
Ship Lake—92, 106

"Ship Lake Pass"—105-106
Skilak Lake—*41*, 42, *43*, 47
Skilak Lake Lookout—42-44
Skyline Trail—44-46
Smith Mill—164
Snowbird Mine—133, 135
Soldotna—48
Sourdough Creek—154-57
Squaw Creek—149-151
stream crossings—18, *19*
Suicide Peaks—102
Summit Creek Trail—*62*, 63, 64
Swan Lake cabin (Resurrection Pass)—63
Swan Lake Canoe Route—35-39
Swanson River—38, *38*
Swanson River Canoe Route—35-39
Symphony Lake—118
Syncline Mountain—148-52

Table Rock—93-94, *95*
Talkeetna Mine—141
Talkeetna Mountains—135, *143*, 145, 148
Thompson Pass—163
Thunder Bird Falls—124-27, *125, 126*
Tikishla Peak—111-13, *112*
Tincan Creek—70
Trout Lake—63
Turnagain Arm—66, 67, *67*, 68-69, *68*,
    78, *80*, 90-91, *90, 95, 104*
Turnagain Pass Ski Tour—69-71

Valdez—163-64

water, for drinking—16-17
Wedge, The—106
white water classification—21
Whittier—78-79
Williwaw Lakes—107-109
Williwaw, Mt.—107, 108
Willow—136, 138
Willow Creek—136
Windy Corner—98
Winner Creek—*82*, 85
Winner Creek Trail—81-83
Wolverine Peak—109-11, *110*
Worthington Glacier Overlook—161-63

About the authors:

HELEN NIENHUESER, originally from Pennsylvania, has lived and hiked in Alaska for more than 25 years. She lives in Anchorage where she is a planner for the Alaska Department of Natural Resources. She spends her spare time exploring Alaska's wilderness.

NANCY SIMMERMAN, born and reared in Dayton, Ohio, has been an Alaska resident for more than 24 years; she lives at Girdwood near Anchorage. A professional outdoor photographer and writer, she is also the author of *Alaska's Parklands: The Complete Guide* (The Mountaineers) and *Alaska II*, a large format photographic essay.